REMEMBERING
WHAT MATTERS MOST

Trusting Your Body: The Embodied Journey of Claiming
Sacred Responsibility for Your Health & Well-Being

REMEMBERING
WHAT MATTERS MOST

A CALL TO COURAGE FOR PARENTS

READY TO TAKE A STAND FOR CHILDHOOD

IN THE AGE OF TECHNOLOGY

Susan McNamara

The Healer Within Series

The Farm at
AVALON
PRESS

ISBN 978-1-958611-00-5 Paperback
ISBN 978-1-958611-03-6 Ebook

The Farm at Avalon Press
www.RememberingWhatMattersMost.com

The Farm at
AVALON
A REMINDER OF WHAT IS POSSIBLE

To my family of origin who set in motion a remembering

*To my chosen family who allowed me to
give birth to that remembering*

CONTENTS

The real focus here needs to be on our families, not the technologies.

An Introduction To Remembering What Matters Most

As a child, I lived with the constant and unspoken reality that something was always in between me and my parents. Something was always in between me and my siblings. And something was always in between me and myself. It was not love, connection or protection, but rather an obsession with the wrong thing that insinuated itself into every single aspect of our lives together; from what time dinner was, to how we socialized, to what we did and believed in as children, to how we were with one another and to how we felt about ourselves.

Something non-human was more important than people's feelings. It was more important than health and well-being. It was more important than honesty, self-care and trust.

Ultimately, it was more important than me. A thing told us who we were and how to act. It told us how to be with one another, how to spend our time and what to value.

Sound familiar?

Like any child, I needed to feel connected to others for me to feel safe and seen. Throughout my entire childhood, and beyond, I worked very hard to get the important people in my life to pay attention to a relationship with me. Because what I did never seemed to work, I kept trying harder and harder, believing that the lack of interest was some short-coming on my part. I kept thinking if I could just do or say the right thing, at the right time, and in the right way, *finally*, I would be seen as someone worth having a relationship with. That what had been keeping us apart would finally be set aside.

It never happened.

This left me feeling like there must be something very, *very* wrong with me. That there just had to be some dark and awful thing about me that was keeping the people closest to me from wanting a better connection. That there just had to be some horrible insult perpetrated by all of us kids that the life of our family was secondary to a substance. And because I was told I was causing problems or making things up whenever I mentioned the elephant in the room, I took it to heart. *How could it be otherwise?*

What did I know? I was just a kid. Which is why I believed the narrative that this was all normal. Great, even.

Worst of all, was the choice I had to make over and over and over again; go with the program I was being offered or break from what I was being told, be true to myself and risk being left out on my own. As a child needing to be part of a family, there was only ever one choice for me. I made it as all children must. I chose to put my faith in what I was being given; having no awareness of the personal and relational costs to myself.

The consequence of this childhood dilemma was that for many, many years I believed there was no place for me in the world if I was authentic about what I was sensing and feeling. For too long I was unable to trust myself. And for far too long, I accepted lots of the wrong things as a substitute for what I actually needed. Worse yet, I hated myself and the world when I looked through the eyes of an addictive system. All of this left a deep and dangerous imprint on me, so soul-crushing that I wonder still how it is I did not wind up going over some edge from which there was no coming back.

Growing up in addiction, I traded feeling at ease for being the one in charge long before I was developmentally ready to take that role on. And I got very, very good at it. Because parents in an addictive constellation are MIA, I learned how to do for myself and others at a very young age, how to accept harmful and sub par substitutes and how to go without what I needed most. When I got older, I tried to emulate what I had seen. I drank harder than anyone around me. I took great pride in being wasted out of my mind while still remaining "in control." Just like what I had seen growing up.

When I was "partying," I told myself this was fun. That I was living the good life. Just like the person I most looked up to. Just like the person others looked up to. This added to my confusion. Not only did my own family speak of how great we had it, but so did those around us. But why didn't it feel that way inside of me? If all of these grown-ups, friends and family thought it was so great, it had to be. *Right?*

Back then, when I was sensing and saying that something was off, nobody wanted to hear it. For them to hear would have been to admit there was a problem. To admit there was a problem would be to recognize that something must change, and then actually work to make that change happen.

Today, I humbly stand before you saying something is terribly off in our world. That how we are living and raising our children, what we have made most important and what we are exposing them to through the screen technologies is robbing them of their innocence and squeezing the life out of our families. Because "everyone else" seems to be doing it, we think this is all so normal now. Great, even. Including our children, who look to us for everything, and who are watching our thoughtless, obsessive tendencies with our own devices, and who are believing this is something worthy of emulating. Taken to its natural conclusion, we are teaching our children that machines are what give our lives meaning and purpose, and that being glued to one is what makes for a good life.

Beginning

I begin this book with a deeply personal story because I want you to know why it is that I see what I see and why it is I made the choices I did with my own children. Why it is that when I look out into our world, at all of the emotional, relational and soul sickness being generated by our love affair with all things technology, the destruction I see is not new to me. I have seen and lived all of this before. I know all too well the devastating effects it has on the life of children, our families and our communities when the wrong thing is prized above all else. And I know intimately what happens to a child who is forced to grow up too soon and who goes without what they really need.

Sadly, this is exactly what is happening when we allow our children to be routinely exposed to more than they can handle. It is exactly what happens when the devices are given more of our attention than what we give to the people we love. The "specialness" we have bestowed upon the screens tricks our children into believing that a thing is more important than them, their innocence, their free time, their mental and spiritual health, their connection to those they love, *and so much more.*

While no parent, mine included, would ever, *ever,* want to convey any of this to their children, *this is in fact* what always happens in an addictive system where something, other than people, is given the top priority. This is, in fact, what always happens when we make an outside thing more important than our loving and committed attention to what we value most.

So while the addiction I grew up with was alcoholism, *addiction is addiction.* Meaning, that when the wrong thing is running your life and the life of your family, it becomes the toxic sea you swim in without realizing what you are actually swimming in. In other words, you don't even notice the costs, and if you do, you feel powerless to do anything about it. The fallout of addiction is that you will put up with what is most decidedly abnormal, *without question.* And while it is a slow creep that happens over time and through many, many large and small moments, decisions and interactions, the end result is always the same: A child's belief that disconnection, denial of real human needs, distraction, soul-sickness and isolation is what feels like home.

Is this not exactly what is happening and has been happening in our homes, as we have allowed the technologies to take over more and more of our lives? More and more of our children's hearts, minds and souls?

This becomes more than obvious when we consider all the ways the devices have become inserted into the very fabric of our lives, and into the very core of who we believe we are now. We sleep with it. It comes out to dinner and on walks with us. We are afraid to be without it, or very far from it. We're anxious when we lose it or can't get to it. We don't feel like ourselves without it. It tells us how valuable we are, and whether or not we belong. We go to it for relational comfort when we are lonely and turn towards it to decide how we get to feel about ourselves. We use it to rant when we don't like what is happening and to anonymously attack those on the "other side." We wield it as a shield between us and loved ones when things are not going well. We use it for shallow self-disclosures and narcissistic dumps. We turn towards it for what to believe in about the world and ourselves. We let it serve as a substitute for feeling alive and for living with meaning. And we go to it to obsessively avoid, isolate and self-medicate.

A Hard, Cold Reality

We have yet to develop the proper scrutiny and the necessary boundaries to maintain a healthy balance with the screens in ways that would keep them useful in our lives and in the lives of our children. This is bad news for our families and for the healthy development of our kids. Because we have come to believe our children must have all these technological devices in their lives now to be okay, we can miss what is actually happening. Along the way, the wrong thing becomes "normal" to our children who only know what it is we give them.

Because the technologies so saturate their world, our kids have come to believe this is just how it is now. That this is the very best they can expect from us. Given the undeniable dependency of our children on us, they will learn to be satisfied with whatever it is we bring into their lives. Satisfied with very little, *if very little is what we offer them*. Satisfied with sub par substitutes for love, connection, time in Nature, creativity and more; being led to believe that this is what makes for a good life.

To say the screens are having a devastating impact on our children and on our families would be the understatement of the century. It's clear they have a hold on us. I would even go so far as to say, we are letting them use us, *instead of us using them*. Sadly, we are conditioning our children to do the same. Through our own dependency and unexamined beliefs, we are training our kids to go to the technologies for anything, *and everything*. We are teaching them their personal device is how to satisfy their most basic human needs and wants, that they must always have it with them, and that having one is a symbol of elevated social status. In the meantime, we're allowing a machine to show our children what it takes to belong and to be happy, as we ourselves put those very same devices in the position of serving as a guardian of their safety through all of the tracking we do.

Because our children are being conditioned to believe that living the good life dwells inside of a screen, they grow ever more accustomed to sidestepping the challenges that are inherent in being alive in the real world; opting instead for distraction, making the wrong things important, abdicating their sense of self-worth to "likes" and favoring relationships mediated by the anonymity of a screen. They cannot imagine life without it, and they panic at the thought of not having it. *Sound extreme?* College students of mine regularly reported habitually and unconsciously reaching for their cell phones even when it was not there; feeling *unlike themselves* and alarmed by its absence even though they did not need it for anything.

It is more than clear that for all of the opportunities we have been led to believe technology is affording our children, it is actually failing them in significant and profound ways. It fails them because it occupies nearly every sector of their lives, overshadowing what it is that children truly need to grow well. Even with mounting evidence around the downside of technology in childhood, including increased rates of depression, anxiety, narcissism, addiction, isolation, sleep deprivation, academic problems, behavioral issues, suicide, decreases in attention, loss of empathy and self-esteem, along with alienation from friends and family associated with the use of the technologies, *we continue to let our kids live at the mercy of the source of all of this suffering.*

Given the enormity of what we face, of what it is that hangs in the balance for humanity, I propose we begin with the startling premise that **the screen technologies are most decidedly beyond us.** I know this is a big statement, *and a big ask.* To begin with such an inconvenient and shocking truth is a bold, decisive, visionary and courageous step to take. For to admit that the devices have gotten away from us is to begin the essential journey back to re-instating what it is that matters most in the life of a human being. Contained within this gargantuan perspective leap is everything we need to bring about a more thoughtful and balanced perspective to a culture mesmerized with all things screen.

Personally, I believe that by looking squarely at what we have been avoiding, ignoring and denying, we open ourselves up to the necessary painful recognition and reconciliation of what we have let slip through our fingers when it comes to childhood innocence, well-being and a life based on our values and our time together. While not easy to do, *what you do here as a parent matters.* Our children are always watching and sensing us; with our words serving as a distant second to what we actually do. So while we may believe our children know what is in our hearts about them and what we value, if our attention is focused on a device, that's what we tell them is most important.

If our children grow up seeing us care more about something else other than them, they *will* feel to their very core there is something unlovable about them. If our children grow up without the necessary protection they require, their childhood *will* be marred by overexposure to content that is harmful, degrading and nonsensical. And while in the busyness and distractions of our lives it may feel easier to sidestep looking more deeply into the messages you are sending your kids based on how the devices are being used in your home, it will *always* be far less fulfilling, honest and real when we choose to avoid the real life consequences of the bargains and the trades we are making with the screens.

You As The Parent

Modern parents have grown accustomed to believing that others know better than we do. That the experts, the schools and the culture at large have the answers for us when it comes to what we should be agreeing to around the technologies. This has caused us to doubt our most basic and necessary parental knowings around how to raise our young. And it leaves us vulnerable to the belief that we need a steady stream of outside sources to tell us what to do. **But the reality is, you are the only one with the built-in know-how around what is best for your child.** The only one who will be around to witness the impact on your child's life long after educational programs, new initiatives, the latest technological iterations, marketing campaigns and your children's "friends" have come and gone. *You* are the only one in all the world that holds both this honor *and* this sacred responsibility.

Which is why learning to trust yourself as a parent calls upon you to embrace the questions, as opposed to looking for easy answers. This requires leaning into those things you might sometimes seek to avoid, while learning to be deeply suspicious of quick solutions; opting instead to take the long view. *As in the lifetime of your child.* This approach is never about adhering to any specific doctrine, philosophy, influencer or expert opinion. Instead, it is about the transformative potential in learning how to be a parent who taps into timeless and heartfelt truths around what it is that human beings most need in order to live well. It is about being the one who has decided to get clear about their values and actually live them. And it is about being the one who has opted to live in the present moment as the truest place to figure out what to do next.

With that said, you do not need more information or research studies. Frankly, our children's childhoods do not have the time to wait for the next research study to publish its findings. More to the point, we already possess within us all the information we need. An inner knowing that is born out of what we are sensing and instinctively feeling as a parent comes built into us. Guidance that is readily available to know how to act on our children's behalf is pre-installed.

Contrast this to the fact that we have more outside information than we have ever had as a species. Simultaneously, we are sicker and more confused than we have ever been. This is good news. *Why?* Because it shows us definitively that relying on outside information is not how we change, and because it serves as the rationale for why it's time now to turn back towards trusting ourselves as parents instead of letting all the "expert" voices out there pull you in a hundred different directions.

To do this requires more presence on your part. Your ability to be here, now. It also requires your willingness to ask difficult questions. This kind of work will demand that you learn to separate your ideas and values from what your parents told you about the world and about who you are. It will ask you to become aware, vigilant even, about what the marketers are selling to you and your family. It will mean learning how to step beyond your fears and the culturally condoned neurotic, obsessive helicopter parenting style that far too many of us have embraced in lieu of a present and authentic relationship to our children. And perhaps, most difficult of all, in order to be with such powerful and probing questions, you will have to learn to slow down, sit down and listen more deeply than perhaps you ever have.

The Power of Love

The good news is, everything you need is built right into you. And it can be summed up in one word: Love. There is nothing more powerful than the love and the devotion parents have for their children. It feeds us with passions and capacities we did not know we had. It gives us courage, focus, endurance and vision. *This is something we all possess.* This is something we can all learn to tap into regularly and consciously in order to decide well on behalf of our children and our lives together.

The power of love was something I didn't know anything about until I had children. And then it blew me away. I had no idea I had such strength, clarity and foresight built into me until I became a mother. This is the force that guided me as I raised my children, and it is the place from which the heart and soul of this book was seeded in the decades I spent raising two children to adulthood. *This is something we all have, and this is the place from which I speak to you now.* From the heart and soul of a mother and from a woman who still remembers acutely what it was like to be a kid, and to have your heart broken and your soul crushed because the adults around you had bought into the wrong thing.

So while I have a Masters Degree in Psychology, am ABD at the Doctoral level in Clinical Psychology, have trained in alternative approaches and have professional work experience with children, it was only after becoming a mother that I really knew what kids needed beyond what I had ever learned in school. Equally, it was only through mining the losses of my own childhood that I was able to fully understand what kids truly yearn for.

While you will hear some of the specifics of my own journey into the power of love, I am not here to prescribe anything to you. I am only here to say, *there is another way.* A way I found that is based on learning to be more present so you can choose more clearly and more wisely. A way based on doing the challenging work of figuring out what you value most in Life and then living accordingly. A way steeped in discovering what it is that kids truly need that transcends the pull of the times.

Did you notice, as I did many years later, that none of what I just said has anything to do with the technologies? That's because to do right by our children and our lives together has got absolutely nothing to do with the screens. As a matter of fact, when we make the devices the central focus in our lives, we rob ourselves and our children of the joys and the necessities of life as a fully functioning human being.

That's why this is not a book about how to hack your way into a healthy relationship with the screens. There is actually no such thing. Whenever we make the screens the center of what we are doing, and how it is that we can fit our lives into them, we are starting in the wrong place. The starting point must always be how it is we most want to live and what it is we most want to gift our children with. Which is why for the title of the book I chose *Remembering What Matters Most* to serve as an anchor for what we want to base our lives on. This is vastly different than figuring out how to rearrange ourselves and our children to fit into the world of the technologies in a more "balanced" way.

The Exploration

Woven throughout this book are the three guiding forces I described above when I was proposing a way to live based more fully in the love we feel for our families. This is what I turned to when it came to what I did and believed in as a parent trying to do right by my children in very challenging times. To be clear, this exploration is *never* about demonizing technology, nor is it about deprivation. Instead, it is about discovering and creating a way of life for our families based on *what matters most to us* as we learn to trust our undeniable place as the one in charge of our child's life. We would totally miss the mark if we made the focus be technology, and how it will improve (or not) the lives of our children, keep them safe, make them progressive or be the deciding factor in their friendships and social status. Instead, the *real focus* here needs to be on our children and our lives together. The *real focus* needs to be on what we value most. The *real focus* needs to be on what it is that supports and nourishes a developing human being.

To that end, below are the three fundamental orientations, or ways, that guided me in my attempt at raising kids well and creating a home life based on what mattered most to me. They are:

1. Learning How To Be More Present
2. Getting Clear About Core Values
3. Recognizing And Honoring Real Human Needs

Each one of these is a world unto itself: An ever-expanding and ever-revealing powerful North Star to help you navigate through even the most confusing and challenging of times. Each fundamental orientation is given its own chapter, as well as being woven throughout this book. Supporting the three fundamentals are stories and experiential sections to help you, in your own way, get to what matters most to you. These are not scripts to follow, but rather guideposts to help you explore and experiment. My hope is there will be many moments where you will say to yourself, "*I knew that.*"

Finally, it's essential to point out this is never about being perfect. As a matter of fact, striving after perfection when it comes to raising our children will never be good enough simply because it creates inauthenticity; generating guilt, overwork, competition with other parents, inner tension and the pursuit of all the wrong things for all the wrong reasons. At its best, we make room for ourselves as we grow into the knowing of what we value and who we are as a parent. This includes making room for the inevitable ways we will all make mistakes with our children. Times where we will not get it "right." Times when we will be unsure and confused. Times when we will go down the wrong path. Times when we will forget and times when we will go on to remember. It all gets to be here because this is Life and the living of it with all of its complexities, confusions, challenges and mysteries. And because there are no ten "perfect" easy steps to the complex journey of guiding and protecting another human being.

A Sacred Call

It has been a long, and at times, arduous journey to grow into being able to answer the sacred call of motherhood. Before children, I had no idea what would be asked of me or what it would take to live out my values in the day to day in a world that does not protect children. Nor did I know back then that I would take what I had learned and offer it out as a book to others. But here I am, having come to the place of raising children into adulthood, while finishing a book that has been nearly twenty years in the making. I hope I've done justice to what it is I've discovered and lived. And I hope I am brave enough and clear enough in the writing to be sufficiently vulnerable with you in terms of both what is being lost to us, along with just how much power and capacity you have to decide what is best for you and yours. I pray that what is written here helps you do what you need to do in order to become more present to your family's real needs, while you figure out a way to live your values. And while there is no guarantee when it comes to our kids, I can tell you one thing for sure: If you make the focus of your life be on what you love most, you yourself will grow into the kind of human being who can help guide their children towards their most extraordinary selves, all while answering the sacred call to be a Protector of Life.

Your capacity to be
here now is what makes
you a trustworthy
source for your child.

1
Being Here Now

"Wherever you are, be there totally."
Eckhart Tolle

In May of 2015, I got an emotional call from my father telling me my mother had been diagnosed with stage four ovarian cancer, and was to be operated on the following week. The news and the diagnosis came in fast and unexpected. Suddenly, I was making plans, rearranging my schedule and booking a flight to Florida to be with my mother during her recuperation from surgery. You would think that being blind-sided in this way would only be awful. Overwhelming. Frightening. Heart-breaking.

Before encountering the practice of mindfulness, I would have said the same.

But as the experience with my mother unfolded, there was nothing awful, overwhelming, frightening or heart-breaking about it at all. I know this may seem inconceivable, or even callous. But it's neither. Instead, what I experienced was a kind of clear, calm, centered compassion that was completely present to what was unfolding. A kind of presence on my part devoid of fears, drama or negativity. And I owed it all to more than twenty-five years of practicing the art and science of mindfulness.

Before that phone call from my father, I had seen the power of being present play out in my life with my own children and in the challenging decisions I was making on their behalf. Through the practice, I was regularly able to find a clear and centered place to go to that allowed me to connect with them, my values and the demands of the moment as a new parent trying to make her way. But never before had I experienced the strength of the practice as powerfully as I did during the time I spent post-surgery with my mother.

Instead of fretting, fearing, anticipating and wringing my hands, I centered my days around a rhythm my mother and I naturally established together. She would get up in the morning, and because I had not been awake all night due to anxiety over her, I easily and automatically woke at the same time she did. I would make her a little food after which she would go back to bed. Then, I did my practice, went for a walk or a run, or maybe out to get food. And because I did not spend those times away from her conjuring up worst case scenarios, some obsessive story about how bad things were, or that I had to be on guard and ready to be available 24/7 otherwise something horrible would happen if I wasn't there, I found myself going through the day in the most easeful and restorative of ways. This left me grounded and with lots of energy; available to be present to whatever it was she needed of me, as well as being able to easily care for myself. This as opposed to draining myself by focusing on me, my fears or distorted stories about how I needed to be available.

What did this look like in action? When I was out walking or running, instead of feeling like I needed to hurry up and get back, I let myself feel the motion of my body and the air on my skin. When I was food shopping, I let myself enjoy something I love to do. When I was doing my morning practice, I let myself sink into the support of something that deeply holds me. And then, much to my surprise, each and every time I would be finishing up with whatever I was doing, *at the very same moment*, my mother would be waking up and walking out of her bedroom. It was absolutely uncanny. Stunning in its effortlessness and synchronicity. Inspiring for its total absence of anticipation on my part. It felt magical and divinely guided, and it held me in ways large and small. And when it came time to make decisions concerning the food she was eating, how much she was moving or what kind of pain management she should use, I set aside all of my own ideas, all of the thoughts I had about what she should do or how I would do it, and instead, I tuned into what she needed and what made the most sense to her around health and healing. I did this over and over again. Moment by moment. It was a profoundly connected, peaceful and sacred time for both of us. One that we continued to speak of and to cherish in the years to come.

When I returned home, everyone assumed I had been through a harrowing, grueling experience and that I must be exhausted. This could not have been further from the truth. I came back rested and immensely grateful for the connected time we had spent together. Time that was not marred or distorted by my fears or my need for things to be a certain way. It was one of the greatest experiences I have ever had of being present for and with another person, of accepting the reality that stood before me and of finding beauty in the midst of what most people would believe could only be unwanted, terrifying and overwhelming.

I tell you this story because this is what is possible when we practice being more present, and because this capacity is available to all of us. I would go so far as to argue this is perhaps the greatest skill you can develop as a parent seeking to make solid, visionary, value-based choices when it comes to what you and your family need to be healthy, balanced and prepared for the future.

Getting Real

No matter where you fall on the spectrum of opinion around technology in our children's lives, it's impossible not to notice that *it is* changing them. The very essence of what it means to be alive is being redesigned, reworked and renegotiated as generations of children spend increasing amounts of time in front of a screen. The impact it's having on them has wide ranging effects from how they think about themselves and the world, to how they relate to one another, to how they spend their time, to what is happening to their physical and emotional health, to their ability to get a good night's sleep, take care of themselves, pay attention in school and *so much more.*

In a game that is always changing, in a world where the decisions a parent has to make daily are mind numbing in quantity alone, in communities where we can no longer assume that what we choose will be supported by our neighbors, schools and our children's friends homes, **wouldn't it make sense to develop skills that would allow us to be present to what it is that supports healthy children? Wouldn't it be wise to find ways to assess the true cost of technology's presence in our homes?** *Wouldn't it be prudent to explore all of this in a way that goes beyond anti-children agendas, special interests, our own fears and hang-ups and the ever-changing landscape of expectations that are out of keeping with the healthy unfolding of a child's life?*

And wouldn't it feel great to make choices based on what your kids really needed, as opposed to being enslaved to the dictates and seduction of a machine's influence on you and your children?

I think one of the biggest obstacles to knowing what to do as a parent and one of the biggest drains on the energy we need to make solid decisions for our kids, are all of the over-exaggerated dangers we conjure up in our minds, all of the future tripping we do about what will happen down the road, and all of the ways we allow ourselves to be weakened in our role because we fill our minds with critical and undermining self-talk. It goes without saying that what it takes to be a parent has always been overwhelming. Factor in cell phones, video games, apps, social media, educational requirements, entertainment, music and more and that experience intensifies; leaving many of us feeling powerless and ineffectual just trying to keep up with it all. *Is there something then that can serve as a source of real wisdom and true guidance in our attempts to evaluate what is best for our children, and that goes beyond our fears, anxiety and critical self-talk?*

Becoming Mindful

Being present moment to moment without judgment is what Jon Kabat-Zinn calls the art and science of mindfulness—the practice of learning how to be here *now*. The practice of learning to suspend choosing for or against what is happening; opting instead to learn how to be with whatever is *actually* happening. Both inside and outside of you. This way of being is, at its heart, about observing yourself and your surroundings as you move through your day, doing what you are doing, thinking what you are thinking and feeling what you are feeling. This includes noticing how often your mind is not where you are; either stuck in the past, or anxiously anticipating the future. Mindfulness is about observing all you see and experience; acting as a witness to, an observer of, the reality that exists before you, *and within you.* From this state of mind, you are in a better position to see more clearly what is truly happening, and therefore, what is truly called for when it comes to all the decisions you are making as a parent.

Being mindful requires your attention, along with a willingness to learn to be with things as they are. *This is not an easy thing to do.* Especially as a parent confronted with raising children in a world pushing a seemingly endless array of things that children need now; with the cell phones and other devices leading the charge. Not to mention how many of these choices have never been properly vetted when it comes to health and safety. Not to mention how many of these choices have less to do with the real needs of children, and more to do with profit motives and so-called "progress." It's hard to know that though when you're caught up in your own distractions, what everyone else is doing or what your child is pushing for.

This is where mindfulness can come in—opening you up to greater insights into how and why you choose as you do. Being present in more ways and in more situations in your life helps you recognize just what it is you are relying on to influence your most important decisions. *And isn't that exactly what we need? To understand why we are choosing for our children the way we do?*

Learning to pay greater attention to what is actually and truly happening for our kids and what they are being exposed to, instead of believing what we are being told, or what we want to believe because it is just too inconvenient to know otherwise, puts us in a position to better guide our children. For when we can learn to be in the present moment more often, noticing the truth of our experience, some things just become undeniable and irrefutable. And if we can be brave enough to stick with what we discover, over time, we begin to learn that we can trust what it is we are seeing, feeling and knowing. Even when it is difficult to do so. Even when the way forward seems muddled and unclear.

Practicing being more mindful to your thoughts and actions helps you to disentangle from all of the made-up dangers, both from within and without, by landing you right in the clarity and truth of the present moment. From there, it's so much easier to be with what comes up in Life because you're not making things up, or worse than they actually are. And because your not using someone else's ideas or opinions as the basis for your decisions.

Withholding Judgment

It's essential to point out here that choosing to be more mindful would be cruel and overwhelmingly difficult if we did not also learn to identify, question and suspend, the judgment that arises. For when you begin to notice more about yourself and how you operate as a parent, *you will see and feel* all kinds of things that are normally pushed beneath the surface of your awareness. Things like the toll late nights on their cell phone is taking on your child's mood and ability to concentrate in school. Or the fact that social media is leaving your child seriously depressed and even hating themselves. It may also be something like noticing how addicted you are to your own phone or that your family prefers the screens to each other. In these moments, it is natural to want to overlook what is painful. To deny what is happening. But that doesn't mean these things aren't there. It doesn't mean these things aren't robbing you and your children of what matters most.

But if you can be brave enough to be with what you are noticing, you begin to re-learn how to be more present and how to see things like judgment, criticism and any "unwanted" discoveries as sources of important information. (I say re-learn here because the ability to be present is inherent in who we are). So if in these moments you can tap into what is inherent within you, you become more aware of what you typically keep at arms length. In so doing, something will begin to shift for the better in terms of understanding yourself and your decision-making process as a parent.

Practically speaking, this might look like labeling what you are noticing, saying *softly and kindly* to yourself, "judgment," "criticism," "unwanted." This will help to ease the experience and allow you to stay with the process for a moment longer by creating some distance and objectivity. Judging ourselves or avoiding what is hard shuts down the learning and the process of discovery that is available to us when we choose to stay with what we are noticing. Avoidance of this kind keeps us from knowing the truth because feelings like guilt, shame, self-loathing and inadequacy that show up when we feel less than our best as parents, are such painful experiences that we will go to great lengths to avoid them.

Which is why intentionally cultivating non-judgment creates the space you need to look more directly at things and with more clarity—especially when what arises makes you feel afraid or like a bad parent. To be clear, noticing what is difficult doesn't make the situation worse, or even mean these thoughts are true. Instead, it brings to light what is already there, but that you typically deny or ignore. Despite the protection we think it affords us when we push things away, even if we are not aware of consciously doing this, whatever we push down will drive our choices and behavior. Whether we know what drives us or not.

That's why labeling the judgment, or any other difficult thoughts or feelings for that matter, puts you in the elevated position of understanding why you are making some of the choices you are making as a parent. This then empowers you to step beyond needing to be governed by, or buying into, what does not serve your life. *Or the life of your children.* For our purposes here, being more mindful helps you to see when the use of the technologies helps, *and when it hurts.*

While it can initially seem counterintuitive, turning towards the challenging moments of parenting with awareness can serve as guidance about what in our lives is off kilter. If we can learn to pass through these difficult times without turning away from them, so much becomes possible for us in terms of how to navigate the world on behalf of our children because we are not using up our energy denying what stands before us. Being more mindful allows us to become the one who can see through the hype, the pressures, our own blind spots and straight to the heart of what it is that children really, *really* need. From this place, we are less likely to be fooled, pressured, misled or guilted into anything.

Stuck In The Past Or The Future

It's also important to point out that while we were all born with the capacity to be present, our conditioning and our life experiences have taught us to dwell more in the past or the future. Our ability to recognize exactly what is needed in any given moment cannot, *and will not*, ever happen in the midst of past or future thinking, busyness, mindless activity, stress, overwhelming schedules or the justifications we engage in around how we need to use the technologies. *Why?* Because when any of this is happening, *we are not here.* We are, in fact, MIA. And when a parent's presence is missing, it is far too easy for the wrong things to take hold. Far too easy to make decisions based on flawed information.

Because here's the truth: **How could you ever know what your child truly needs when you are looking through the distorted lens of future worry, past conditioning, overwhelm or distraction?** How can we *possibly* know what to do for our children if we are not actually *right here?* Here is the only place we can decide from, and is the only place where our children are being impacted. The present moment is the only place, *ever*, where we can see clearly what is happening. This is different from all of the "what-if's" or the "what we don't want to happen" or "what we think we have to do" scenarios that so many parents use as a filter to raise their children.

Our children do not need our hyped-up and exaggerated fears and anxieties. Nor do they need a parent who is so consumed with busyness and distraction as to be partially in attendance. Instead, they need us fully here; assessing what is happening in a clear way and making our choices for them from that place. So instead of being somewhere else, aim to be where you are as often as you can and watch what happens to your insights, your perspectives and your decision-making. There is no right or wrong to this, and there is nothing to achieve. This is about you being right there with what is happening. Learning from it and letting yourself make adjustments based on what you are discovering. This is different from reading about it, being told about it by another, hearing from an expert, or even being driven by your own past or future thinking. This is the direct experience of you noticing your child hunched over their screen and monitoring their moods versus listening to your pediatrician tell you what you should do based on what the American Pediatric Association screen time recommendations are.

A Long-Term Practice

Becoming more mindful is not something you do once and then you've mastered it. This is a daily, moment-by-moment commitment to being with things as they are. In other words, it's all about practice, practice, practice. *A lifetime of practice actually.* A long-term, lifelong decision to learn both the ins and the outs of what it takes to locate the mind in the here and now.

It stands to reason then, that while starting up a practice of noticing your thoughts can feel like a lot of effort to begin with, in the long run, it is far less work than what we typically do; whether we recognize it or not. For instance, *how much effort is it to live anxious, guilty or irritated over the constant petty fights you have with your kids over their phones? How much judgment is associated with spending more time on the computer than you know is good for you? How much angst is generated by allowing your son to have the video game he says everyone else has, even though it feels wrong to you?*

Isn't getting caught up in all of the reactionary ups and downs of your thoughts and their consequences, in and of itself, a great deal of work? Maybe even believing that this is the best you can hope for when it comes to how you parent? Some semi-explosive kind of living where you swing from one uncomfortable mental and emotional experience to another? Left unmindful of your thoughts and motivations, you're a victim to the habitual tendency of the mind to be somewhere else. This leaves you out of touch with what is happening right now, as well as creating a lot of extra work and misery. Not only is this deeply unsettling for you in terms of how it feels to be alive, it leaves your children without an in-charge adult present enough to see what needs to be done in terms of what they are being exposed to via the technologies.

The practice of mindfulness requires nothing from you in terms of money, gear or time. You do not need to schedule time to practice. Or pay someone to teach you. Instead, it is a matter of placing your attention on whatever you are doing, wherever you are, however you are, and whoever you are with, *and noticing that.*

Final Words: The Power Of Presence

If there was only one thing I could have done raising my kids, it would be the practice of mindfulness. Learning how to pay more attention to what was both inside and outside of me grew a deeper connection to myself. That meant I was more grounded, more clear and that I had somewhere to go when I felt lost or overwhelmed by difficult thoughts and feelings. Being more mindful is also what supported me in discovering what my values were; the ones I most wished to impart to my children. The ones that were different from what I got growing up, or what it was that the commercial culture was insisting upon. Finally, being more present more of the time helped me to see my children for who they are, not who I wanted them to be.

When we choose to pay more attention to our lives, a kind of inner peace begins to settle over us as we spend greater amounts of time in the present than we do in the nerve-racking future or the habitual stuck-ness of the past. Choosing to be more present creates a kind of openness to all kinds of situations, difficult ones included, that defies what we might predict in terms of what we are capable of or what an outcome might be. It can feel almost magical in terms of what is possible when we bring all of ourselves to the moment.

This is a welcome relief to the stories we create in our own minds that are based on self-generated fears, insecurities, confusion, anxiety, past worries, future anticipations and more. And it gives us the confidence we need, moment by moment, to challenge outside sources like technology companies, government mandates and commercial and societal pressures that are not in keeping with what our kids truly need. Seeing your life through the lens of the present moment is an act of immense courage, determination and loving commitment. Everything you need in order to be a trustworthy source for your child when it comes to what you allow into their lives, as well as what you don't, is based on your capacity to be here now.

An Inquiry:
An Existential Question

Try noticing yourself for the next week whenever you find yourself in front of a screen. As if you were watching a movie of yourself, notice how often, *and why*, you find your way to a device. *What prompted the choice? Avoidance? Distraction? An end to boredom or other difficult feelings?* Get in the habit of regularly asking yourself, *"Why am I here?"* whenever you find yourself in front of a screen. And then listen. *Really listen.* This is not an opportunity to judge yourself for doing something wrong, but instead a chance to bring some clarity into how you use the technologies.

Anything and everything you discover here will help you to know better how to support your children. So for you and for them, try getting very, *very* curious about yourself as you engage with your devices. Watch yourself from a distance, as if you were a character on a stage. Whatever you see here holds an essential key for how to navigate the screen world for yourself, and by association, your child.

To be clear, this exercise is *purely* about noticing. There is no right or wrong here. As in, *"I shouldn't be doing what I'm doing"* or *"I'm doing it all wrong with this mindfulness thing."* This non-judgmental approach remains especially true when you discover over and over again that your mind has set up all kinds of reasons for you to find your way to a device out of habit. Give yourself a break by recognizing that each time you catch your thoughts about why you are choosing what you are choosing, you are now back in the present moment again. This means you are no longer on automatic pilot. Meaning, instead of the screen being in charge, *you are*. Now you have a choice.

Finally, the idea of asking *"Why am I here?"* came from a college student of mine. One semester, while we were working with mindfulness and technology use, one of my students took a sticky note, wrote that question down and stuck it to the back of her phone. That way, every time she picked up her phone out of habit, she paused to really assess her choice. It took me two months before I realized she had posed *the most central and existential question any human being can ask of themselves: "Why am I here?"* In other words, will I allow my life to get reduced down to a relationship with a machine, or do I want more? *And do I want more for my children?*

A Practice:
Seeking Your Own Counsel

When you begin to pay more attention to life with the technologies, you might just notice how the fast-paced demands of the machines stands at odds with the slower pace required in making thoughtful decisions for your children. How being rushed and forced into the next thing leaves little time for a measured response. And how being pressured as a parent to make a decision you're not ready to make, rarely, *if ever*, makes for a good outcome.

Not to mention the tension it generates in you, along with the strife and the arguments it sets up in your family.

Begin to notice how often you feel rushed or pressured into a choice around the technologies and your children. Pay attention to the thoughts and feelings that come up. Listen to the arguments being made for why it has to happen right now. Become aware of external pressures to line up with others. Notice where you feel tension in your body. Pay attention to the atmosphere these moments create in your home.

Staying mindful of it all, begin to explore what it would be like to wait. *What it would be like to wait until you had the time to sort it all out? What it would be like to value your child's childhood enough to slow things down?* Wonder to yourself if waiting might be the very best choice you could make for your child at this time, knowing that if it is right at this moment, it will still be right one week, one month or one year from now. But if it is not right at this moment, and they get involved with it, *it will never be right.*

With this in mind, make a commitment to yourself, and to your family, to get in the habit of saying, *"That's not a decision I feel ready to make just yet. I need some time to think about it."* And then carve out some time alone to seek your own counsel. A time when you can tune into everything you are sensing. Ideally, this is something you have set up in your life on a regular basis, not just when there is a crisis. That way, you'll be comfortable with checking in with yourself, understanding its value.

This doesn't have to be fancy and is as readily available to you as turning off the music and podcasts while you're driving or cooking so you have some time to think. It can be time in the shower or over a cup of tea in the morning. Take it to a journal or to a good friend. What matters most here is that you give yourself the space you need to make a decision based on your values and the needs of your child. Every moment spent in this way will gift your children with greater protection and care. Therefore, make it a point to regularly create some unscheduled breathing room for yourself as a foundation for making calm, wise and visionary choices for your kids.

Potent Questions

There are so many ways we unconsciously use our devices, especially now that they go with us everywhere we go. Which is why, if you want to use the technologies, *as opposed to them using you*, get in the habit of asking yourself some penetrating questions to help wake you up to the present moment. For instance...

- *Am I using my phone as a shield to intimacy when I text instead of call?*

- *Is my screen use revving me up? Is it making me feel anxious or depressed?*

- *Am I afraid to be without my phone? Do I obsessively check it?*

- *Do I have trouble getting off a screen even when I know I "should?"*

- *Is my cell phone the first thing I reach for in the morning and the last thing I touch at night?*

Practical Go-To's

To deepen into the practice of becoming more mindful, there is nothing more present than your body. Your mind will go off into future fantasies or into what happened in the past. But the body always lives in the present moment. So while our minds will justify and rationalize all the reasons why we need to check something or answer something, our bodies will always, *always* tell us the truth. Therefore, begin to notice your body in relationship to your time in front of a screen.

- **Notice your body more often.** Your face. Your shoulders. Your head. Your back. Your eyes. Try saying, *I am aware of*...to really hone in on what you are experiencing.

- **Pay attention to your sleep.** Do you lay in bed with texts, posts, images and theme songs rattling around making it impossible to fall asleep?

- **When in front of a screen, stay in touch with your body's most basic needs.** Thirst, hunger, comfort, pain, the need to go to the bathroom and the urge to move are all essential pieces of information you don't want to ignore. The screens go 24/7, but a human body does not.

- **Pause for a moment before getting in front of a screen.** Take a breath. Get clear about *"why now."* What are you *really* looking for in this moment? Does your use fit your values? How about the role modeling you want to do for your kids?

- **Pair mindfulness with parts of your schedule.** For instance, see where your mind is at upon awakening, or before you go to bed at night. Driving, cooking, brushing your teeth, walking the dog, showering, getting your kids out of bed in the morning are all great examples of anchoring yourself in the daily rhythms of your life as a way to remind yourself to come back to right now. Get in the habit of asking, *"Where am I right now?"*

- **Be intentional when you're in front of a screen.** Be aware and deliberate when typing, swiping and clicking. Do not engage in or encourage speed. Opt instead for a steady and relaxed pace.

- **Keep things human when you are using a screen.** Look out the window. Go outside. Get on the floor and stretch.

Our children
count on us to take
a stand for them.

2
Claiming Your Authority

*"But as far as I can see, most parents of my generation-
from the tail end of the Baby Boomers to the tender tip
of Gen X-don't really rule the roost. We sort of scratch
around it apologetically, seeking consensus."*
Susan Maushart

In the span of one month, I heard disturbing stories about two lovely young girls, both fifteen at the time, and both of whom I knew.

The first story involved one of the girls sexting with a boy who was not her boyfriend, or even a potential boyfriend. This girl had not experienced so much as a kiss. Yet here she was exchanging naked photos of herself, along with lewd comments she likely had little to no idea the full meaning of—all at a time when she was right at the beginning of exploring her budding sexuality. Perhaps worst of all, she was telling her worried friends that what he was sending her and what she was doing, "was no big deal."

The second story involved another young woman who started a texting relationship with a much older boy she had met only once. Early into the exchange, the young man became sexually inappropriate and aggressive in his texts to her. Her friends sent a text asking him to stop. *His response?* To text back, telling this young girl that if she told her friends any more about what he was saying, he was going to find her and sodomize her. She too, had never so much as been kissed. *Her response to all of this when her friends challenged her?* She dismissed it by saying it was nothing to worry about because "it was just a text."

For weeks after hearing these two stories, I could not sleep. I sobbed whenever I thought of these two girls and what was being lost in terms of their innocence. What was being taken from them via these screen mediated exchanges that would never have happened so easily in person. And I was enraged at a world that would create and allow such a thing to go on. I felt frustrated and ineffectual. It felt like there was nothing I could do. Or so I thought.

One day, I shared my desperation and outrage with my college classes. I told them the two stories in great detail without hiding how overwrought I was. Much to my surprise, you could have heard a pin drop. The students were riveted. Yet when I asked if any of them were shocked or outraged, or if these stories were new to them, *not a single hand went up.* I went on to ask this question for a number of semesters in a row to literally hundreds of students, and still, *not a single hand went up.* Not one of them saw these stories as rare, unusual or even much to get worked up about given how common they'd become.

But somehow when they saw my unfiltered reaction, when they saw how distraught I was, something changed in them. They began to open up about how they were being impacted. Through witnessing my outrage, they began to access something they had been denying and it left them unable to look away from the devastation of what had happened to these two girls. By association, they could not ignore the impact these same kinds of experiences were having on them and the people in their lives.

In subsequent classes, I went on to tell them about how my family was living at the time. No cell phones. No TV. No social media. No laptops or iPads. I told them how we were raising our children with little to no technology. They were amazed, curious, and at times incredulous, that my children could be doing so well socially and academically without what they believed was a "must have" in childhood and adolescence. Somewhere in the midst of this ongoing dialogue, they began to talk about their anxieties in trying to keep up with it all. They spoke of their dissatisfaction with their relationships via their cell phones. They openly discussed not being able to sleep at night due to the ever-present pull of texting and social media. The women in class lamented how the over-availability of porn had left them believing the wrong things about intimacy and their bodies.

I was floored by their candor and the struggles they had kept hidden. Through all the many conversations with literally hundreds of students, I never once lost track of how much the older generation had let them down by leaving too much up to them at too young of an age. How so many of the grown-ups had been bamboozled into believing not only that children needed the devices, but that they could handle everything that came with them.

Based on these initial conversations, I created a curriculum pairing mindfulness with their technology use to help the students explore the role the screens were having in their lives. Much to my surprise, many of them came to class talking about some pretty big changes they had made. Like getting off social media. Like spending time with friends and family without their cell phones. Or one of my favorites—noticing that when they were studying and they put their phones away, they were more invested in their work, and their grades improved.

Theses experiences with my college students are ones I will always cherish because they reminded me that the younger generations look to us; despite what they might say, what we might assume, or what we have been led to believe from marketers who have convinced us that children should be left to their own devices in order for them to fit in and keep up with the times. And these times with my students taught me that the human spirit is infinitely creative when it receives the support and the inspiration it needs.

In the end, and perhaps most surprising of all, these young adults openly worried to me about the generations to come, and how they felt bad for the kids today because they felt their childhoods were being lost and stolen through social media, gaming and Youtube obsessions. Interestingly enough, the very same things my generation worried about in regard to them.

Learning To Be The Gatekeeper

Our children count on us to take a stand for them. To be the gatekeepers for them in a world offering kids far too much and far too soon. They look to us to be the ones to hold the gate open, or to close it and *latch it tight*. This is something the virtual world will never, *ever*, do for your child.

We as the parent must be the one to represent something of value to our children, while serving as the custodian of their childhood. To do this requires we come to understand and dedicate ourselves in the service of guiding a life. It is a commitment without a guarantee. A sacrifice with no paid benefits. *It is the bond we create with our children born out of our capacity to be the one in charge.* This is not easy to do. Growing into our adulthood as a parent cannot be boiled down into a time frame or a formula. So while there are many systems of thought and practices that can serve as a map for us, the map is never to be confused with the terrain because to answer the call of being the gatekeeper in your child's life is deeply personal work, *and is the work of a lifetime.*

There are so many things to figure out when it comes to taking care of another human being; health, food, sleep, school, friends, schedules, toys, books, sports, routines and more. There are practical and immediate choices to be made, as well as visionary and long-term decisions to be thought through. There are obvious and not so obvious things to pay attention to. *All of which must be decided by you.* And all of which lay the foundation for the life of your child. Given the enormity of this, it's obvious why it's impossible to boil this down into a quick fix approach.

But *it is* through the meeting of all of these choices and challenges that we as parents begin to gain a sense of who we are in the life of our child; while building the credibility of our sacred role and responsibility *one decision at a time*. This is the very bedrock out of which authentic and life-affirming parenting flows. This is never to be confused with perfection, guilt, blame, or doing more. Instead, it has everything to do with the recognition that **you are your child's first, most enduring and most important protector and role model.** Your children count on you to keep out of their lives what is not good for them. They count on you to teach them the preciousness of their existence and therefore, *what is worthy of them.*

An Unhealthy Inversion

Unfortunately, our role as the gate keeper in our children's lives is being seriously and dangerously undermined. A disturbing trend of *leaving it all up to the children* has got it all backwards; turning the necessary hierarchical nature of the parent-child relationship on its head. The truth is, *it is up to us* to decide for our children, for a *very, very long time*, what comes into their world, *and what does not*. The unprecedented and disturbing trend now of children being in charge puts our kids at great peril for they lack the cognitive and emotional maturity to make decisions of such import.

The evidence of this inversion is everywhere. We let young toddlers decide if they need a nap, or when to go to bed at night. We let our school age children decide how many devices they have access to and how many activities they will be involved in. We let our teenagers dictate how much time they will spend texting, what they will do on social media sites and how late they will stay up at night engaged with all of this. This inversion has even begun to extend out into the systems we interact with where the medical world has created portals for our children's healthcare that denies us access without a *minor's* permission. This is nothing short of outrageous in its overreach, and is a devastating undermining of our role.

Instead of parents deciding what their kids will be exposed to, we have outsiders, along with children themselves, dictating what they get involved with. In the inversion of the parent-child hierarchy, the grown-ups have been pushed to the periphery by our own confusion, the pressures of billion dollar marketing efforts, persuasively designed devices, influencers and by our own children's peer groups who they turn to now instead of us.

But in order for our children to be adequately protected, and for our families to remain healthy and intact, we must stop asking the children what we should do. We must stop seeking their permission. We must stop leaving decisions up to our children that are beyond their emotional and mental abilities, and instead, *reclaim our place as the ones in charge.* The ones who understand what a growing body needs and how to meet those needs in healthy ways. The ones who say *this is what comes into our home and what does not.*

And the ones who stop looking to outsiders to give us permission about the decisions we make for our children.

While many of us would say that it's us, of course, who decides, that it's us, of course, who's in charge, *is that actually true?* Pay close attention to where you let your children decide. To the cajoling or the haranguing that you cave to. Or where it is you let your guilt decide. Or where it is you allow peer, societal or marketing pressures to decide. Or where it is you let systems like schools, the government or medicine decide.

Putting yourself squarely in the role of the one in charge will require your time and your dedication to understanding what motivates you, along with what it is you are allowing to go on with your children. Without this level of awareness, we can lose track of our sacred responsibility to them in the "limitless" world of technology, *forgetting that childhood requires limits.* Demands limits. Begs for limits. **In the Age of Technology, we have forgotten there must be a regular and consistent presence willing to set and hold the necessary boundaries and limitations that contribute to a healthy childhood.**

Without this remembrance, the most basic impulse of every parent—the drive to protect and do right by their children, is undermined. Without this instinct intact, our parental expertise becomes compromised; leaving a gap in our capacity to choose well on behalf of our kids.

And in that gap a void is created. One that is more than easily filled by something else. Today "that something else" translates into "all things screen." Which then translates into the hearts and minds of our children being shaped and consumed by something non-human— whose agenda has got nothing to do with their healthy development.

Think about it. Do you really want a technological platform, an app, the seduction of a cell phone or images on Youtube being what's in charge of your children? If not, *what is it you want in charge of their hearts, minds and souls?* If you can learn what this is and then learn to stand behind it, you will be well on your way to being the one in charge of the life of your child.

Parental Disempowerment

The fact that so many of us are struggling when it comes to the technologies in childhood begs an essential question: **"Why are so many well-meaning parents not in charge when it comes to the technologies and their children?"**

As I see it, there are many things fueling our disempowerment. For starters, our built-in parental guidance systems are being hijacked by marketing strategies that focus on separating parents from kids. Companies and entertainment vehicles do this by depicting parents as out-of-date, out of touch and in the way. *Somehow incompetent.* This dangerous and deviously crafted lie may be a boon to the bottom line, but it is pure poison for our families when the adults are portrayed as irrelevant, or even comical, in their ability to know what their own children need.

Then there are our own addictions to the devices. Caught in the throes of our inability to regulate our own use, *how can we possibly help our own kids?* How can we possibly model something for them that is life-affirming? Your capacity to get a handle on your own use plays a huge role in your ability to stand as the empowered one in charge who can make solid decisions for your own child. Added to what I have mentioned above are all of the distractions, busyness and exhaustion that compromise our capacity to live fully as the gatekeeper. Under the sway of these things, we just want our lives to be easy, convenient and free from additional work. Enter the screens and their ability to keep our children occupied, quiet and entertained, and we have the recipe for the screens taking our place as the ones in charge.

Finally, we also have to include just how much we don't want to be the parent doing things differently. How unimaginable it can feel to make decisions contrary to what "everyone else is doing." What I have to say about this one is that you are not here to answer to everyone else. *You are here to answer to your children and to your own self as the one ordained to be in charge of guiding and protecting a life.* The bottom line is this, I have yet to meet a parent who in some way or another is not worried about how social media, gaming, cell phones and online anything is impacting their children. And yet, it often goes no further than that. For while parents may lament what is happening, or complain about how bad things have gotten, simultaneously we live as if our devices are valued family members who get the preferred seat at the table. Worse yet, allow in that family member we do not even want around our children. So if you hear yourself lamenting about what is happening, but still find yourself ineffectual at *really* doing anything about it, look more deeply. Be more mindful. Something must be at play for you to feel the way you do, and still be unable to make such an important and life-giving choice for your family.

However you decide to do it, find approaches, guides and practitioners that help you get clear about who you are as a parent. Growing into this capacity is something that must be lived, experienced and learned from. Let yourself be compelled to live as your child's protector as fully and completely as you can. The process of growing into yourself and claiming your position as the one in charge of your children will leave them well-prepared for life, deepen your relationship to them, and allow you to let them go with faith and with confidence when the time is right. Along the way, you grow into someone worth knowing as you develop a level of character strength you didn't know was possible.

Protection Is Not Deprivation Or An Excuse To Be Neurotic

To be clear, being the one in charge who can set necessary limits, is *never* about deprivation. Nor is it about being a helicopter parent where you allow irrational fears to drive your choices. It also is not the false argument that we are old-fashioned, controlling or somehow in the way of progress if we refuse to allow the screen technologies into our children's lives without question. Questioning what we are being told, and what is good for our children, is a necessary prerequisite for protecting them, and is the main criteria for being an effective gatekeeper.

But our ability to question effectively what is happening with the technologies can get tripped up, and is heavily influenced by our own conditioning, our ability to think critically, our comfort with stepping outside of herd mentality, how much we are addicted to the information we receive across a screen and so much more. Which is why part of getting clear about your role as the one in charge is to look more deeply at your own childhood. Perhaps you were overexposed to content or conversations that were too "adult" for you to understand. If so, this is something that would leave you now unable to see when your own child is being overwhelmed. Maybe you were the grown-up in your childhood home and now you have a hard time recognizing when you are expecting your child to be older than they are. Maybe you were taught that the world is a dangerous place and so you constantly fear for your child's safety—leaving you to believe they are safer inside in front of a screen. Perhaps you are someone who has always been a people pleaser or who feels that others know better than you. Which is why you defer to what other people say and expect of you.

If what drives our decision-making is left unchallenged, we run the risk of making important decisions for our children based on unconscious fears and old conditioning. The net result being, we don't see clearly what we need to do to protect them. For instance, my husband, who was exposed to movies as a child that were well beyond his years, initially had a hard time knowing what was appropriate content for our own children. This was because, in his mind, screen time overwhelm was mixed up with feelings of connection with his father.

This is not a moral issue of right and wrong according to some narrow definition or religious philosophy. It is, instead, a common sense and natural approach to understanding our essential and non-negotiable role as the protector of our children's innocence. Which is why spending time getting to know ourselves and what we value, what is developmentally appropriate in the life of a child, and what each moment really calls for, is what this is all about.

Protecting our children is not about good or bad or parenting according to the latest book or meme. Protecting them is never about abdicating this responsibility to someone else. What real protection does demand though is that you show up, work on yourself and take your place.

Setting Limits

Which brings us to limit setting. Our children need a more compelling, consistent and benevolent force in their lives than what comes across a screen. At its best our limit-setting creates the conditions for this to happen, and is born out of our values, the needs of the moment and the developmental requirements of childhood. Taken together, this is where we walk our talk.

Our children want nothing more than to be in relationship with grown-ups who love them, *and who know how to draw a line.* This is not done through telling them, or reminding them of this. It is accomplished by our actions, and through our daily choices. This is never about being a tyrant. Instead, this is about knowing what needs to be done, *and doing it.* It is about holding your ground even when your children are unhappy about your choices. Or when the external pressures of a world less interested in innocence and more interested in selling you something, insists upon something for your children you do not feel good about.

This brings us to an important point. Just because your children bash up against a limit, *does not mean you are doing something wrong*, that it is bad for them, or that they can't handle it. Their bumping up against a limit is one way our children know they are safe and protected. While it does not always feel that way to us, or to them, it is true nonetheless. Children *are* going to push back against our rules. Count on it. This is both necessary and good. There will be arguments and disagreements. There will be things you will struggle over and grapple with. This is normal. As a matter of fact, it is more than normal. It is downright required to raise healthy children.

The things in life that are the most valuable are worth struggling for. Worth setting limits over. **Setting clear and enforceable boundaries around how, when and if the devices are a part of your child's life not only sets them up to be successful in other areas of their lives, it protects them in ways they cannot protect themselves.** *When we are not clear and consistent in our limit-setting, it sets up the opportunity for the wrong things to take hold; for a gap to appear that our children will exploit, and from which miscommunication, frustration, bad behavior, poor choices and anger will arise between us.*

Setting limits is not ever left up to our children *for very, very good reasons*. They do not possess the life experience or the judgment necessary to make decisions of this magnitude. That includes their ability to handle effectively the addictive pull of the devices. They need us to do that for them. And if we don't draw that line, *how will they know how to do it for themselves?* You can absolutely count on them being pressured as they make their way into the world. Do you really want to send them into the world not having experienced clear limits? Do you really want to send the message that when they're pressured they should cave to that pressure?

While in any given moment it can feel like too much to do to hold the line, it is actually far more difficult to *not* do the work up front with your children. When we try and get out of what needs to be done we wind up talking more, setting more limits, arguing more, feeling angry and frustrated more as well as doing more clean-up work. When we avoid creating an up-front structure where there is a person who is in charge, fairly and consistently creating limits and setting boundaries, we ultimately create a life our children cannot be successful in. And if they cannot feel successful in the day-to-day living and management of life, they will feel ineffective and be ill-prepared for the world. When we promote inconsistency and absenteeism in our guardianship, we sign them up for becoming human beings who are difficult to be with—those who have trouble with self-regulation, feel entitled, struggle with perspective-taking and lack understanding about the cause and effect of their own behavior. This alone, is a powerful rationale for learning how to set effective and protective limits.

Final Words: You As The Trustee Of Life

When my children were around four and six, I allowed them to watch one hour of PBS on Saturday mornings. Up until that point, it had been a rare and carefully chosen video, or infrequent times at the grandparents where they could see something on public television.

The truth is, I made this decision for one reason and one reason only: I was feeling pressured about my choices, and uncertain about whether or not I had the right to be the one in charge of what my children saw. I kept hearing how I was too strict, and could see how uncomfortable others were around our mostly "no screen" choices. So even though I was passionate about not raising my children on the junk images, values and beliefs as delivered by a screen, I caved in. Even though I felt strongly about protecting their innocence and their right to their own minds and bodies, free from harmful influences, I said "Yes" because, after all, *it was only PBS*.

This little "experiment" lasted a couple of months. My two kids, who were typically good friends and very good to one another, changed after being in front of one hour of PBS. When the show was over they would be dissatisfied with what they usually loved. And they would fight. This was not normal. Normally, they got along. Normally, they had more than enough to interest them. I watched this for a while. Finally, one Saturday after the show was over, I pointed out what I had been observing and asked them what they thought was happening. My daughter saw it too but didn't know what was causing it. My son, in his man of few words way, merely said, "I don't know. I just feel mad." Kaboom! That was it. I did not need a research study. It did not matter that it was "only PBS Susan, for God's sake!" All I knew was that somehow my kids were different, *and not for the better*. And so ended our "little" experiment. A friend summed it up best when she said "I let them watch because I think it will give me a break, but then I spend the rest of the day putting them back together."

What I did not know back then that I know now is that it was through the difficulties, the insecurities encountered and the push back I got from others, that taught me how to trust myself to be the one in charge. This was something I was not aware of in the mid-1990s when my first was born and our culture was at the height of its love affair with all things technological. Because the few voices back then challenging the use of technology with children were unknown to me at the time, I had to find something within myself to rely on. The basis of that being getting clear on what I valued and what it was that human beings needed to grow in healthy ways. The sheer act of finding what to put my faith in, separate from what was around me, grew me as a person like nothing else ever has.

As a parent you are a trustee—someone who does not own their children, nor their future, but who guards and protects them until they reach a level of maturity where they can take up their own lives. As the gatekeeper, if you don't feel good about what is happening with the technologies, you don't have to keep going in a direction that does not feel right to you. You can *always* pause, reassess and reroute. You are, after all, the one in charge.

Finally, as a culture we expect things to be quick and easy. There is nothing quick, easy or guaranteed about taking your place. Your way will take time and be unique to you. It will be different from what others believe you should do. There will be ups and there will be downs. Successes and setbacks. Clarity and confusion. Times when you feel unsure of yourself. Times when you will find yourself in the void of not knowing what you can believe in. This is to be expected. Taking your place as the one in charge means allowing for the unknown. It means learning that what you can trust is available to you moment to moment, and that all that it takes is your attention, plus a willingness to listen, for your best parental instincts to come forward and make themselves available to you.

An Inquiry:
How Comfortable Are You With Saying "No?"

This is as good a place as any to talk about your comfort with saying "No." If you were being totally honest, what comes up for you at the thought of needing to set a limit? Is this something you dread or feel ineffectual at? Do you fear a confrontation? Is there guilt, anger or frustration over having to draw a line?

Merely hearing the suggestion that we need to include more ways to say "No" to our children can leave some of us feeling ill at ease—believing perhaps that drawing essential, life-promoting boundaries is the equivalent of deprivation, denial and therefore, bad parenting. But think about it. *What message do you send your child when you say "Yes" to something they know you do not think is good for them?* Deep down, how do you think this makes them feel? Forget about the fact you just sidestepped your guilt, an argument or a melt down. *What are you actually saying to them when you say "Yes" when you really should be saying "No"?*

This is such a rich place to explore as a parent. For when you look more closely at your inability or reluctance to say "No," guilt, fear, exhaustion and your own childhood are often what you will find. Perhaps there is guilt you are not doing enough. That you don't spend enough time with your kids so you substitute your presence with a device. Maybe you fear if you don't give them things, they will be left out, or that it will demonstrate to others you are not a good parent. Perhaps you're overwhelmed and don't have the strength of your convictions when the going gets tough because you're so exhausted. Maybe you're so fear-based you believe a device will protect them.

But if you can lovingly and fairly delve into what it is that keeps you from using "No" appropriately and protectively, you're in a position to return to a more powerful and effective understanding of your role. This allows you to more readily sort truth from fiction. In so doing, you reclaim the power to choose wisely on behalf of your child in a more confident and effectual way. And when you are more secure in your position, your kids gets to relax into the knowing that someone has their back. That someone sees them as valuable enough to protect.

A Practice:
Before There Was "No"

Consider what comes *before* "No." Before there is even a need to draw a line, we can set up our lives and our homes so that the technologies are refreshingly absent and unavailable. Just like junk food. If you don't have it in the house, or it is not readily available, there is less to say "No" to. No lines to be drawn. Nothing to get into, and therefore, nothing to negotiate or fight over. No frustrating arguments or limit-setting required because it is *just not there.*

While we do not have ultimate control outside of our homes, we do within our own four walls. Therefore, what could you do in the life of your child to make the need to say "No," obsolete? Or at least, less frequent. For instance, how can you tuck the devices out of the way so they are out of sight, and therefore, out of the mind of your child? Can you create more tech-free spaces? How about having less overall devices, and therefore more need to share?

Would you ever consider pausing streaming services for certain time periods as a reset or as an experiment in understanding the impact it has on your family? How about creating house rules where there is nothing at the dinner table, nothing when you are traveling together in the car, nothing in the bedrooms at night when it's time to sleep? How about not allowing violent video games to be available in your home?

If you can get creative here you will not only reduce unnecessary struggles, you will open you and your children up to a world of saying "Yes" to all of the good and necessary things Life has to offer.

Potent Questions

Posing powerful questions can be a real game-changer whenever you want to explore more deeply how you're living. Open-ended questioning helps you get to the root cause of where you might not be showing up as your most in-charge self. Experiment with the questions below to start a process of examining what might be interfering with your ability to fully take up the mantle of being the one in charge.

- *How does your busyness, exhaustion or distraction get in the way of making challenging decisions that align with your values and what you know your kids truly need?*

- *How do your struggles with your own screen use keep you from seeing clearly the impact your child's screen use is having on them?*

- *What fears do you hold about your child?*

- *What beliefs do you hold about what it means to be a good parent in terms of not "depriving" your children of what they want?*

- *Is it easier for you to be your child's friend rather than the one in charge?*

- *Are you so saturated with media messages that you have unconsciously and unwittingly agreed to do things based on what the commercials are selling you?*

- *Where do you allow the devices to be your child's storytellers, babysitters, teachers, friends and authority figures?*

Figuring out why we have forgotten to be the ones in charge requires a willingness to ask some thoughtful, and even provocative questions. Each one of these questions is a long-term exploration in and of itself. Choose one to work on. Perhaps even the one that most ruffles your feathers. Anything that brings up a strong charge in us as a parent often points to something worth looking at. Therefore, if defensiveness or resistance comes up with any of the questions, *look more closely*—you may just find the key to why you struggle to take up your role as the one in charge.

Practical Go-To's:

- **You decide if and you decide when.** It is your responsibility to set clear guidelines and stick to them. At their best, the rules you create arise from your values, the true needs of your child and the requirements of the moment.

- **Be willing to change with the times.** What a toddler needs is different from a baby and different from an adolescent. Because their needs are always changing, so too is the way you live your role.

- **Set healthy limits.** If your kids do not have something to push up against, you are not doing your job. A good parent-child relationship will hold the griping, complaining and boundary bashing your children must do in order to grow and in order to see for sure that someone is in charge.

- **Walk the talk.** Whatever influences you, influences them. You cannot expect your children to do what you yourself cannot.

- **When in doubt, do nothing.** Your kids might accuse you of putting things off. They might be irritated. It might not be convenient. But it sure does make for some quality decision-making on your part to pause for as long as you need to in order to establish yourself in the role of the one in charge who knows how to decide what's best.

- **Make technology permission-based.** Set limits in age-appropriate ways. You decide what goes on in your family because only you hold the larger picture about your values, what your kids need and what is appropriate for your home.

- **Your house, your rules.** This includes when others come over. No need to be uptight about this. Instead, make it a beautiful offering you extend to others.

- **Explore "No" and "Not Yet."** "No" is a complete sentence and is a prerequisite for fully saying "Yes." "Not yet" demonstrates you understand the unfolding nature of your child and the necessity of waiting until there is a developmentally appropriate readiness.

- **Never as a reward, avoidance or babysitter.** Rewards have a way of backfiring and of creating a conditional existence where our children believe they must be rewarded to do what just needs to be done. Allowing screen use as a way to avoid a fight or a difficult encounter makes for ill-behaved and difficult to be around children. Allowing the screens to regularly babysit your child may give you a break, but you have traded your comfort for their well-being.

- **Live all in.** In your temporary role as their guardian, what would it look like to be all in? This has got nothing to do with buying things, driving them all over kingdom come, signing them up for everything offered or obsessively hovering over them. Instead, it is to be with them, and it is to give of yourself.

- **If you would not agree to it in real life, do not agree to it in the virtual world.** Nothing more needs to be said here.

- **An Affirmation.** Shifting your ideas about your role means breaking from old ways of thinking. In support of yourself and what you are growing into, try the following: *"I know what is best for my children and I follow through on that knowing. I am the one in charge."*

At the core of a child
trusting a parent,
is a parent trusting
themselves.

3

Trusting Yourself

"Just trust yourself, then you will know how to live."
Johann Von Goethe

In 1995, I became pregnant with my daughter Madeline. I remember being upset with friends who had already given birth, believing they had not sufficiently warned me about what an absolute and total upheaval having a baby would be. I do not exaggerate when I say that everything, *absolutely everything*, I had ever believed in, got called into question. It culminated for me in what St John of The Cross called "The Dark Night of The Soul"— a total existential breakdown. An absolute questioning of everything I believed in about myself, others and the world. I felt overwhelmed, abandoned, confused and screwed up. I had no idea that bringing a child into the world would so tear me to pieces. But it did.

I could feel the weight of the impending responsibility. I could feel the deadly press of all the unexamined places in my own psyche; the dark and shadowy realms that I knew would be brought to bear on this child, ultimately affecting how she would feel about herself. I knew this all too well through the personal toll my own family of origin's unconscious and unaccounted for dysfunctions had born upon me.

Out of this immense personal upheaval came a shocking realization: *Our culture does not value Life, and therefore, it does not protect its young.* I saw this repeating across all areas of our lives; medicine, food, education, how we treat the environment and more. It showed up as the toxins in the food supply and the poisoning of the Earth, along with the one-size-fits-none approach to health and healing. What this meant for me was that daily I had to choose between society's version of what I was told was "normal" and needed to be in my children's lives, and actually doing right by the real needs of their bodies, minds and souls. This created an inner conflict and tension that left me feeling as though there was something wrong with me— something deeply flawed and contrary in me because I could not, and would not, accept what was being offered in terms of how to raise, protect and nourish my children.

I clawed my way through that first year with my daughter and then less than two years later with my second child,

Jack. This continued through all the years of my children's childhood as I sorted through what it is that children really and truly need. What it is they need to be healthy. What it is they need to become who they are most meant to be. I did not know a lot then about what kids really needed, but by mining the losses of my own childhood and by being present to my own children, I made those discoveries one bloody, painstaking and joyous revelation at a time. As I gave birth to them, I gave birth to myself and we were born together into a home where we all deserved better.

What did that look like? It looked like change, and lots of it. I scoured everything, and I do mean everything that came into their world. I researched, intuited and contemplated health care and food, cleaning chemicals, vaccines, plastics, commercial influences, screen time and more. I continually wondered how to raise them respectfully and lovingly while remaining the person in charge. I challenged myself day after day to own up to what I brought to the table in our interactions; rooting out any projections I might be inclined to impose upon them. I also began the arduous journey of figuring out what my values were, and then of finding ways to live those values into the world. As the days and months went by, I slowly began committing to a daily personal practice as my way of sorting out who I was, and what it was that mattered most to me.

Looking back now I can see how little I trusted myself in the beginning. How vulnerable I was. Every time I encountered someone's negative response or some unthinking cultural mandate, I would question myself and my right to choose what made sense to me. This included my right to make well-thought-out and life-sustaining decisions for my children. Back then I didn't know that what I was doing would sometimes be received as an unwanted challenge to others and to the systems and communities we were a part of. Naively, I thought it would be received with open arms to have a mother looking so deeply into what truly supported Life.

At times I took it personally. But I know differently now. And what I know is this: **No parent should be asked, ever, to choose between nourishing and protecting their young, and fitting in with cultural norms, mandates or expectations.** This applies most especially when a culture is pushing choices that are, in fact, life-depleting and life-negating; poor choices advertised and pressed upon us as "normal," nourishing and necessary.

Despite any pushback I got, I kept going. My enduring focus became my children growing up knowing they mattered and that they belonged to something truly life-affirming. I wanted them to know this, not through my words or through the big, splashy moments of life, not through gifts or by how much I drove them around or worried about them, but through the daily choices we were making as a family, and through the home life we were creating together.

Though not easy, in the end, something miraculous happened. I learned to trust myself. And by learning to trust myself, I sent the message to my children that they could trust me.

Self-Trust

To be a parent, confident in the decisions you're making, is to develop a deep and abiding trust in yourself. A kind of trust that allows you to check in with YOU first. This gives you the courage to stand in the presence of powerful expectations and even demands, and still choose based on what you know is right. Learning how to trust yourself gifts you with a faith in yourself that exceeds anything coming across a screen. But it does require a willingness to release and transform old, destructive habits and beliefs that were passed down to you from your family of origin, as well as from the culture at large. The result being, a kind of timeless wisdom you can rely on to guide you through the most confusing of the virtual realities we all encounter.

That's not to say it's easy to go against popular beliefs and norms. There is effort required to challenge the status quo, along with our own limiting beliefs when it comes to what we should trust. *But it is possible.* I know because when I started, I did not know what to do or what would happen. I went day by day, age by age and school year by school year. I did it without much research to back me up. I did it without the support of the culture at large. And I did it all by embarking on the journey of learning how to trust myself, and by leaning into the support of my husband, close friends and inspiring, transcendent of the times, resources. This is something that is available to all of us when we can be mindfully present to what we are experiencing, and use that as the basis for trusting ourselves.

The "Instinct-Injured"

We are what Clarissa Pinkola-Estes calls "instinct-injured." For our purposes, what she means by this is we have forgotten how to trust our parental instincts. How to rely on that which is natural and innate. Screen messages, "expert" advice, stress, busyness and the sense that we as parents are not doing enough has created, and continues to compound this injury, leaving us vulnerable to the belief that we need a steady stream of outside sources to tell us how to raise our children. *The result being?* We have lost our way with ourselves. And because we have lost our way with ourselves, we have lost our way with our children.

The good news is, our parental instincts are something that is built right into us and can never be taken away from us. We are mammals after all. We have an animal nature and all animals instinctively know how to protect and care for their young. All mammals have ways to tune into their environments in a way that allows them to navigate through unfriendly and unsafe situations. It is only the modern day conditioned mind, subject to what's coming across a screen, that has forgotten what it is we can rely on to safely navigate our surroundings on behalf of our children.

Inside each of us are the instincts needed to make healthy choices for our kids. It does take work though to remember how to trust this. How to tap into a kind of discernment that has nothing to do with relying on some *thing* or some *one* outside of you to tell you what to do. How to recognize where and when you give over your authority to someone else (including your own children). So while at any given moment you may believe it is "easier" to leave it up to some outside source, or to turn away from what feels like too much, this does not mean that the issue you are facing has been resolved. This does not mean that your children have been properly protected. The reality is, any lack of healthy instinct on your part strips you of your parental authority and the self-trust in your decision-making that is a must for ushering your children safely through the world.

An Inside Job

Learning to develop self-trust is an inside job; one that requires tapping into your inner knowings, instincts and intuitions. It is an ongoing process requiring your time and commitment, along with *lots of practice.* This can feel impossible in a culture that encourages us to look outside of ourselves for answers and for confirmation as to how we are doing. After all, teachers, school administrators, politicians, other parents, the culture at large, marketers, our kid's peers and our very own children say they must be digital natives now in order to fit in, to be successful and to be prepared for the 21st century. We are continuously inundated with external information about how to raise our children, from sources ranging from the benign to the opportunistic. This can leave us feeling that others know better about what we should do. And because most of us have had no formal training in child development, it magnifies the sense that it is "natural," or at least easier, to follow the rules, ideas or influence of someone else.

But the truth is, your ability to safeguard and guide your child is built right into you, and it relies heavily on your ability to trust yourself. Our *single most important job* then is to turn inward towards ourselves, and to develop the courage and the capacity to act from this place. A place that is beyond external agenda-driven influence. A place that is beyond old habits, insecurities and the past conditioning that gets in the way of seeing what it is that our children *actually* need.

But maybe you think you know nothing about what it means to trust yourself; having never considered what it would take, look like or feel like. Maybe hearing this leaves you with the belief that you're not up to the task. Maybe trust was broken with you when you were young and so you never established a sense of trust in yourself. Maybe you are currently so busy, frazzled and screen addicted yourself that you do not know where or even how to begin. Or if you even have the strength to begin. Maybe it just feels easier to let someone else be in charge of your life.

All of this and more gets to be there because learning to trust yourself is about starting exactly where you are. Though difficult at times, starting from within and from precisely where you are at is the most accurate and truthful assessment of where you actually are, what it is you need and how to proceed. Here's where your mindfulness practice comes in. If you can learn to get more present, *without judgment*, to wherever you find yourself along the instinct-injured continuum, you are at the most perfect starting place for you.

The payoff can be felt right away when you make the determination to start with yourself *first* before checking in with anyone else. And while there will be many times when it feels daunting, confusing and even overwhelming to do so, if you can remember that your children count on you, your wisdom, your experience and your intact instincts to know what they truly need, it can give you the strength and the clarity you require to step into the unknown territory of looking within, while learning to trust what it is you find there. Engaging with your life in this way will bring you all the confidence and empowerment you ever dreamed of, as well as the tenacity to keep going when you feel lost or when the stakes feel too high.

While all of this is necessary and strengthening, it's hard work. We live in times where there are so many ways to not have to feel or deal with what it is we find difficult or uncomfortable, that we have collectively lost the grit we need to meet Life with all of its challenges. This cultural avoidance has undermined our capacity to mature fully into autonomous adults who can raise their young with strength and fortitude. Just look at all the ways there are to numb out—from alcohol to shopping to scrolling to streaming services to drugs to online gambling to porn and more. Each and every one built to keep you from having to feel what it takes to mature into that autonomous adult.

Then there is the constant push to accept "expert" opinions as the central authority in our lives. Experts we readily turn to to assuage our fears; believing that without being told what we should do, our children would be in great peril. Or that we would stand out as bad parents. Add this all up and we have the recipe for umpteen ways to not take full responsibility for the choices we make; to not do the necessary work of learning to trust ourselves as adults. We cannot afford this, and neither can our children. The consequences of the technologies are already dramatically changing what it means to be human *right before our very own eyes.* Many of us do little to nothing because we don't believe we can trust what we're seeing. Or we do not trust we have the right to make a choice that is different from those around us.

Un-Learning & Gut Checks

Learning how to trust ourselves must include un-learning all of the ways in which we are *not* trusting ourselves. The ways in which we have been diverted and distracted from the truth of what we know on a basic instinctual level. Therefore, on your journey of self-trust, it's essential to figure out what it is you have come to believe that is getting in the way of you relying on your instincts. For when you can identify what keeps you from leaning into what you know to be true, you can begin to dismantle what blocks your flow of inner self-trust and the wisdom that comes with it.

This means noticing when you're getting tripped up by decisions around cell phones, gaming and social media and becoming aware of the beliefs and ideas you have bought into that are interfering with your parental instincts. Beliefs around what kids need to be successful, our desire to fit in and be seen in a certain light, unfounded fears, pressures from family and friends. There are all kinds of things that can get in the way of our capacity to trust ourselves. **But if we can remember that at the very core of a child trusting a parent, *is a parent trusting themselves, we can overcome even the impossible.*** For if we ourselves do not see and trust our own abilities, wisdom and inner guidance, how do we expect our children to? And if they cannot trust us as the most significant authority in their lives, who will they turn to? *A screen? Another inexperienced being in the form of their friends? A platform trying to grab and keep their attention? A company trying to sell them something?*

To make your way through all of this is to support yourself by carving out and committing to a regular time and space where you get to show up, *exactly as you are,* in order to do a "gut check." It doesn't have to be a long time and it doesn't have to look like anything other than what makes sense to you. The only criteria is that you do something regularly that puts you in touch with your thoughts, feelings and inner sensing of what is happening in your life, and in the life of your child. A space that allows you to have all of your feelings. A time you can look forward to in order to tune in and set things right for yourself and your family.

In this space, you do not need to have the answers. As a matter of fact, getting in touch with yourself in this way will generate a lot of questions. This is normal. Questions will let you know you are on the right track. *Why?* Because given that we are in the midst of an unprecedented experiment on humanity when it comes to the impact the technologies are having on our lives, *doesn't it make sense there should be something here to wrestle with?*

It does not matter how, when or where you do it. *Just that you do it.* Maybe it's a formal practice like yoga or meditation. Maybe it's writing in a journal. Perhaps it's rising before everyone else and sitting at your kitchen table with a cup of tea and your own thoughts. It could be going for a walk where you just get to be with yourself. And it is always as accessible to you as turning the radio off when you're driving so you can be with your own thoughts and feelings. So whatever it might be for you, *do something and do it regularly.* Consistency is key when it comes to checking in with, and learning how to trust, your own gut.

Final Words:
Make Room For What You Know

While there were many changes I made in our family's life, for the longest time I thought the thread that I was following was just about my children's welfare. But some number of years in, I began to recognize that through my efforts at learning how to be more present, while claiming my role as the one in charge, something very deep was shifting inside of me. Some undeniable inner call to return to myself and what it was that I knew from the inside, was revealing itself in more and more powerful ways as the years went on.

So while I got into what I was doing for my children, I do believe it was also a way to call me forward into the woman I was always meant to be. The woman that I could feel inside of me for most of my life, but had no idea how to access. Without expecting any of it, as I scrambled along trying to learn how to trust the decisions I was making for my children, I grew into a trustworthy version of myself. This has changed everything for me from how I treat myself, to how I relate to others, to what I will and will not get involved with, to what I know is possible.

In the beginning, your inner knowing may show up as a gnawing dissatisfaction with the way things are, a felt sense that something is "off," even if you can't say what, and even when those around you seem okay with it all. It may present more quietly than the everyday busy thinking mind and the noise of the world. It will certainly reveal itself to be slower and more subtle than the speed of the digital highway. While this may initially leave you wondering how something so "little" could possibly serve as guidance big enough to guide your children with, *stay with it.* Even when you are not completely sure. Even when you can't quite articulate it to yourself or others.

Take heart. The information you receive in this way is the domain of instinct and intuition—a parent's purest and most powerful guidance system. We all possess it. *Everyone of us.* It just takes time, trust and experience to know that it is there, to know you can rely on it, and to ultimately, know how to talk about it.

An Inquiry:
Becoming More Authentic

Have you ever considered that when you act against what you know to be right, your children will sense that you are untrustworthy? *How do you think this makes them feel?* Even if nothing is said, even if they get their way, do you think they notice when what you feel instinctively and what you do, are different? What message do you think this sends? Might it erode their sense of feeling safe in the world, or their trust in you to protect them?

While none of us would ever do this intentionally, it's precisely what happens when we ignore the inner voice of parental instinct. When we go against our better judgment just to avoid some inconvenience, we send a confusing message. Whether we intend to or not. Our children are highly attuned to this. As mammals, a big part of the communication from parent to child is on the non-verbal level. Meaning, they are always sensing and feeling us. You already know this to be true if you've ever felt like your kids know you better than you know yourself. That's because they tune into what is below the words. They "hear" the discrepancies and contradictions between our words and what's behind them.

Part of learning to trust ourselves requires noticing when there is a gap between what we're knowing and what we're choosing. Though not a comfortable thing to see about ourselves, this is often where the biggest breakthroughs and payoffs come in as we cultivate a greater sense of authenticity between our instincts and our actions. Doing this allows us to act and feel more unified, more authentic and more trustworthy in our role as a parent. Given this is where we most yearn to be, when you feel yourself outside of integrity, try asking, *What am I denying right now that I know to be true?*

A Practice:
From The Inside-Out

Going from *"What do they think?"* to *"What do I think?"* is an essential and gigantic leap in the journey of claiming your ability to trust yourself. Shifting like this opens you up to the experience of learning to follow your inner signs and signals about how to raise your own children that has nothing to do with what others believe you should do. The more you can learn to do this, the more your confidence grows. The more your confidence grows, the more you align with the truth of your values, the real requirements of the moment and what it is your children really need to grow well.

One way to do this is to find some time when you can be alone with yourself. Sit for a moment just breathing. Place one hand on your belly and one hand on your heart. Then, without thinking too much about it, or worrying about how it may appear, ask yourself, "*What does my gut tell me about my children and…(fill in the blank)?*"

Focus on your body. *Does something grab you in the belly or at the heart? Does something feel tight? Does an image or a memory arise?* Use all of your senses and instincts. Feel for places of tension in the body. Pay attention to emotions like annoyance, sadness, hopelessness, overwhelm or irritation when you picture your child and the choice that stands before you.

Allow what you are noticing to transcend good or bad, what others think, self-doubt or what the marketing images persuade you to believe. Get curious about what you would normally move away from. Sometimes the information you receive may feel vague, murky or unfamiliar. At other times, you may get a sudden burst of insight. No matter what comes up, *stay with it.* There is no right or wrong to this. Nor is it a test you can fail.

Instead, this is a powerful practice to cultivate to put you directly in touch with what you think. The more you do it, the better at it you become. And the better at it you get, the more you'll be able to let this kind of instinct-based guidance inform your decision-making. Along the way, you model for your kids what it looks like to listen to an inner knowing, as opposed to a machine.

Potent Questions

When we choose to take the big leap of learning how to put our faith in ourselves, we need the support of those who understand what we're trying to do. People who get our attempts and who offer a level of feedback that helps take us beyond the doubts and the hesitations. Those relationships that return us to ourselves, while giving us the hope and the inspiration we most need in our journey towards trusting ourselves. It's important to point out that support is different than relying on an external source to do it for you. The deciding factor here being *that you* retain the full responsibility for your choices, while recognizing we all need assistance when we are attempting to grow in new ways.

Here are some questions to help you check in.

- *Who or what helps you to trust yourself?* Do you have this in your life? If not, why not? Is there a way you can imagine getting it?

- *Do you spend enough time in the presence of those people, energies, practices and places that support you?* Who we associate with has the power to strengthen our self-trust.

- *Do you have teachers, authors and practitioners whose work inspires, supports and informs your ability to turn towards yourself?* We all need help from those who can open us up to new possibilities.

- *Do you spend time with people who thwart or undermine you?* As important as it is to find support, it is equally as important to avoid people and situations that ridicule or undercut your attempts to grow and change as a parent.

- *What are your sources when it comes to childhood and technology?* How have they formed your ideas and beliefs about what you do? Are they agenda-free?

Although we may encounter struggles with those who do not understand what we are doing, these encounters can help us to respect that we each have our own way of dealing with the choices we face as a parent. Additionally, if we allow them to, any challenging encounters carry the possibility of growing and strengthening us. Over time we might even begin to see that through our efforts to articulate what it is we are doing to those who disagree or who are unfamiliar with what we're doing, we get a chance to catch up with ourselves, while getting little glimpses of the power of learning to trust ourselves from the inside out.

Practical Go-To's:

Life as a parent contains lots of challenges. The more we can develop inner skills and perspectives to deal with what's difficult, the better off we are, and by association, the better off our children will be. Not only will developing the capacity to be with challenges serve as a source of empowerment for you, it becomes one of *the very* best capacities you can pass along to your kids. Check out what's below to build on this capacity.

- **Make a regular habit of sitting quietly, breathing and noticing yourself whenever you can to lay the foundation for self-trust.** Think of it like a parentheses in the day—a time when you get to *just be.* You can literally do this anywhere; on the toilet, in the car, on a walk, in bed upon awakening or before falling asleep at night. Literally, anywhere you can get just one moment to yourself.

- **Create times of pause when the going gets rough.**
  Let go of the circumstances. Let go of the need to
  react or figure anything out. And for a moment, *just
  do you*. Tend to what you need to do for do yourself
  to bring in some balance before you proceed. This is
  a time where you know that ultimately you'll address
  what needs dealing with, but that for just this minute
  you get to be where you are without trying to figure
  anything out.

- **Be more discerning about who and what you resource
  when it comes to what children need.** Are you relying
  on those selling you something to get your information
  from? Are there hidden agendas? Are the schools
  influenced because of the free technologies they
  receive? Is the so-called "convenience" of the medical
  portals worth what you give up?

You cannot get to a good place by doing the wrong thing.

4

Carving Out Your Values

"But the big things—how we think, what we value—those you must choose yourself. You can't let anyone—or any society—determine those for you."
Morrie Schwartz

When my son was eighteen months old, I was in the middle of the final push to complete, and then defend, my doctoral dissertation. I had less than two months to go in order to graduate that year when I realized there was a major glitch in the way I had collected the data. The problem was fatal enough that I was going to need to throw out a portion of my research. What that meant was I would need to find more women willing to fill out a series of questionnaires regarding their experience of pregnancy. This was not going to be an easy thing to do. I had already spent almost two years finding the women currently enrolled in the study. I had also spent more than four years going to classes, doing an internship, completing practicums and taking qualifying exams.

I had been working harder at this degree than anything else (other than raising children) I had ever done in my life, and I just needed it to be over. To say that the research setback initiated a meltdown would be the understatement of my life. Which is why one day, when I had to go out to the store, and my toddler did not respond immediately when I called him over to get into the car, I flipped out. *And I mean really flipped out.* Enraged, I grabbed him and stuffed him into the car seat. Stunned and terrified, he started to cry. *My response to this?* I started screaming at him—berating him for crying, and telling him this was all his fault for not listening to me. And when, because of how upset he was, he threw up, I belittled him further. It was the ugliest and most violent moment of my life. And when the fugue state of rage dissipated, I fell into a bottomless pit of grief and shame.

When my husband got home that night, he found me holed up in our bedroom. I was inconsolable. As I poured out to him what had happened, I realized that in my attempt to go for the doctoral degree, I had been violating what I valued most—my relationships with my family and a balanced and sacred home life. I felt so derailed. I had been going for something so intently and so single-mindedly that I had not noticed how it was eroding what I cherished most.

Not only was I in violation of my values, my husband pointed out a teensy-weensy flaw in some logic I had created for myself. Despite being trained in a field I actually wanted nothing to do with, I had been telling myself, along with everyone else, that when I finished the degree, *then* I would get into the work I felt most called to—alternative approaches to health and healing. But I wasn't actually trained or training in any of those modalities. Somewhere inside I had talked myself into believing that the "Dr." in front of my name was going to give me some magical entry into that world. In that moment with my husband, I realized I had been using the whole doctoral chase as a defense against taking a chance on going for what I most desired.

The following evening, my family and I built a bonfire in our backyard, and together we burned ten years worth of books, articles, notes and copies of my dissertation. It was a magical moment as I watched my two children dance around the fire. And while many were shocked, incredulous, upset even by my actions, the four of us knew why I had done it. It was my equivalent of Cortez burning his ships when he got to the new world to insure that his crew would be all in. That "little" fire forced me all the way into what mattered most to me. There was no going back. And that is just how I wanted it to be: No going back on my values. No going back on what mattered most to me.

A Value-Led Approach To Your Life

I once heard someone say, *"You cannot get to a good place by doing the wrong thing."* While all of us want a "good place" for our children, we may miss the fact we're doing the "wrong things" to try and get them there. This is not intentional as much as it is a kind of succumbing to our own blind spots that arise out of things like too much busyness, peer pressure, our own addictive screen tendencies, a lack of trust in ourselves, along with all of the ways we are being overly influenced by marketing efforts that tell us what we need in order to have a good life.

On the other hand, a value-led approach to your life weaves together a home where your stated values and your lived values are one and the same. This is easy to state, but harder to live. It does not require anything of us to say we value our children and their well-being or family time. But it does take everything to live that intention, choice by choice, day after day. ***And while initially identifying and living your values can take a lot of work, once you're clear on what matters most to you, the choices around technology (if, when, where and how) become more obvious, more manageable and easier to implement.*** Best of all, your home begins to feel more consistent and supportive of what it is that is most important to you; offering your children a powerful legacy to come back to for the rest of their lives.

This is important in both the short and the long term as your children are keen and astute observers of you and how you do things. *What matters to you, matters to them. What you do, they will do.* No matter what we say, it is how we live and what we choose that determines what our children pay attention to. If this resonates with you, then it only makes sense to be absolutely certain that what you're doing in your home is actually what you want to pass on to your kids. For it is these very same values that will go on to support, guide and insulate them for the rest of their lives. But if your values are missing, or somehow spotty, so will the support and guidance they count on receiving from you.

Your capacity to get clear on what you value, *and then live those values in the day to day*, is what serves to guide you as a parent, and what it is that will protect your children when it comes to the influences of the screen technologies. Identifying the values you want to live by is not a one-time affair, nor do your efforts or the "results" follow a straight line. Living a value-led life is about taking a self-correcting approach to how you live where you regularly check in with yourself to see if your actions are in line with your identified values.

Given what you're asking of yourself and your family (especially if you've been doing things differently up to this point), it is crucial that you practice being as kind, patient and non-judgmental as you can, and that you reach out and ask for help as often as you need it. And if you are ever in doubt about how well you're doing living your values in the day to day, ask your children what *they think* is most important to you. Not to ask permission around what you should do, but as a check-in to see how things are landing with them.

The Argument

While we can all name the advantages of technology, how often does your use, or your kid's use, violate the values you hold? The very same ones you most hope to live by and pass on to your children as a way to navigate the world. The very same ones that serve as the basis of your character and level of integrity. This may be *the single most* essential question we can ask of ourselves in The Age of Technology. A question that when asked and lived can serve as the counterbalance to the destructive influence of the technologies in our homes and on our children's mental, physical and social health. This is a question that when kept front and center in our lives can cut through the confusion, the waffling and the tendency to believe it's okay to set aside your values in the real world for the allure of the not-so-real virtual world.

Are the screens in any way interfering with your most cherished values? If so, you're allowing the wrong thing to be in charge in your home, while sending your children mixed and harmful messages. In so doing, you leave them without a compass to navigate by because the upholding of core values was never appropriately modeled for them when the going got tough. This is perhaps one of the most destructive elements of our addiction to the devices: Their ability to get us to let go of what matters most to us. If this hits home, get into the habit of regularly asking yourself, *"Is this choice in line with my values?"* And if you find that a choice *is not* in line with your values, begin to make the necessary adjustments. Start where it's easiest and build from there. If, however, you discover something that is egregiously in violation of your core values, you *must* start there. It is imperative to let your children know that our most important and sacred values are non-negotiable.

For instance, if one of your family values is non-aggression, but you allow your son to play violent video games, you are out of integrity with your values. If you believe strongly in the power of social connection and you allow your child to be consumed by the dark side of social media, you are out of alignment with what they most need. If you believe your daughter deserves better than to be reduced down to her looks, and you allow her to post heavily curated and sexy pictures of herself online, you are letting her down. If you say you value family time, but spend a lot of time around your children checking, scrolling and texting, you are sending a hypocritical and conflicting message.

What's Not Working

While what I just wrote can be painful to hear, it can be a direct way back into aligning with your values when you can be willing to look at what you typically avoid looking at. You would be surprised by the power of mindfully looking through the lens of what is NOT working. Where you are NOT happy. Where you do NOT feel connected to those in your life. Where you are NOT at ease about what is happening with your children. Where you are NOT satisfied with your home life.

This can seem like a paradoxical approach to take. As people we tend to move away from what is uncomfortable; covering up or distracting ourselves from what is not working in our lives. But if you can muster the strength and the courage to face what feels out of alignment for you, it can become a direct path back to what you value most. Or perhaps even a revelation that you do not know what you value. While painful to recognize when and where we're not clear or consistent around our values—if we can open to what we're noticing, while suspending judgment and criticism, a lot can shift. This is yet another place where your mindfulness practice *really* comes in handy.

If you can mindfully witness what is not working, you begin to see all of the daily choices that do not line up with your stated values. The more you can make room for the time, practice, patience and commitment this requires, the easier it becomes to sort through what you want in your life, and as importantly, *what you do not want*. And if it ever feels as though doing this level of work is more than you're capable of, take a breath and think about your children. Think about what you want for them. Think about what values you want to pass on to them. Keeping them front and center as you pass through challenging insights about how you are living, will give you all the motivation and the courage you need to keep going.

Finally, while it's one thing for you to make this level of commitment, it can be another when it comes to your family. For instance, if you come to see there's been a discrepancy between what you value and how you've been living with the technologies, and you want to make some changes, you can expect pushback from your family and from those around you when you start to do things differently. This can feel hard; especially when you feel that what you're doing is in everyone's best interest. That's why it's essential that your spouse or partner is on board, and that you spend time getting your kids up to speed on what it is you have recognized, and why it is you are making the changes you are. Of course, how much you involve your children depends on their age. But ultimately, no matter the age, *you are the one who is deciding*. Not them.

A Little Caveat

Getting clear on your values can leave you out of step with the culture at large. For when we begin to contemplate which values truly support our homes and our children, we will most certainly find ourselves at odds with certain prevailing modern day norms. Like the ones that push for busyness over a sane home life. Or the ones that make it seem okay to let young children be consumed by content on a screen that is developmentally inappropriate for them. Or the "norms' that insist teens must have devices to be safe and have friends.

While this is obvious enough to state, to be "out of step" with those around us can be very challenging in practice. Our relationships are so essential to us, on such a deep and primitive survival level, that we will sometimes choose to violate our own values just to maintain our affiliations. If you doubt this is you...*How often do you not say what you think, feel or value, for fear of another person's response?* Have you ever made a purchase or allowed something screen-related to go on with your children you didn't want or feel comfortable with, because you were afraid to go against the grain? If the answer is yes, this isn't an opportunity to beat yourself up, but to begin to acknowledge when, where and how belonging to the group is causing problems for how you live your values.

Then there's the flip side of acquiescing to the wrong things in order to maintain our sense of belonging, where we demonize others when our values appear, *or in fact are*, different from those around us. This dicey intersection is reflected on the world stage in divisive hate speech that spans political and religious lines, shows up in our troubled and domineering relations as a country with other nations, and presents itself in the daily difficulties that we ourselves encounter with those around us who do things differently.

To stand for your values is not about staking out your turf and then going to war. To stand for something is to be willing to live from that place, despite what others do, *or do not do.* It is to learn how to live your values while respecting the right of those around you to live their lives as they see fit. It's not easy, but it is essential work if we are to continue on together as a species. Learning to discover and hold what you value without allowing separation and conflict to dictate your interactions with those around you not only supports your home, it heals the world. The personal work you do around this one has the potential to heal riffs on personal, familial, community and global levels. This is truly Gandhi's invitation to *"Be the change you wish to see in the world."*

Final Words: Front End Loading

My husband and I had a concept we affectionately referred to as "front end loading." What that meant for us was we had come to the conclusion that it was far better to put the work in up front when it came to our kids. That the more we could address things head on, and in the moment, the better everyone was for it in the long run. And the better and happier our home life was when we dealt with what came up, as opposed to trying to kick some proverbial can down the road. What this did was set a tone of consistency and fairness with our kids. Because we weren't always changing our minds or having to do clean up because we had avoided something, a kind of trust was built. This lessened the amount of frustration and arguments that might have arisen due to unclear expectations or changing rules.

The very heart and soul of our front end loading was our values. The very same ones we spent year after year calling forward and refining. Living our values only made sense to me if they were strong enough to help us make important decisions in the day to day. *And they did.* Trying to reinvent the wheel each and every time a challenging choice around the technologies came up would have caused enormous amounts of stress and was not something I wanted to be doing. What I wanted was to pass on a legacy to my children they could rely on. What I wanted was a peaceful and sane home life. What I wanted was to protect my children. And that's where my values came in. They did the heavy lifting by giving me something enduring I could return to in order to be guided by what mattered most to me, and what it was I most wanted to pass on to my kids.

There is nothing more powerful and insulating against the times we're living in then to be crystal clear about your values. Your kids need a strong set of values to help them navigate the times they were born into. Ideally, they initially come from you, *and ideally*, you live them day by day *clearly, honestly and strongly*. This is what will support your children throughout their life—gifting them with something sustaining and nourishing to return to when trying to decide how to live. Something that allows them to go beyond the "right" and "wrong" of cultural norms, peer pressure and persuasively designed devices.

An Inquiry:
Do You Know What You Value?

There are so many choices we as parents need to make on a daily basis. Without a clear map of what we value most, we can find ourselves forced to make countless daily decisions on the run and while under stress, with no coherent approach. This leaves us inconsistent and unreliable with our children; creating lots of confusion, instability and hypocrisy. Not quite the legacy we as parents hope to pass on.

Identifying what you treasure most in life is an ongoing process that requires your personal efforts in collaboration with the other adults in your family, your community, and in increasing ways as they grow, your children. This is not accomplished in a single contemplation or conversation, an afternoon, a weekend or even a year. Instead, it is something you live, reflect upon and make adjustments to, *regularly*.

One way to start the process, or to refine what you're already doing, is to carve out time for yourself to review where you are in terms of your values. Write down everything that matters to you and everything you want to pass on to your children. Once you've figured out what you believe, do this inquiry with a partner or someone close to you. Carve out special times to do this when you can be with yourself and another in a relaxed way. (My husband and I would do this once a year and then come together on the beach).

Think of your values as something alive. Something sacred. Treat them as a living, breathing part of your family's well-being; something that requires your attention, commitment and carefully constructed shifts and adaptations. Let your values be a guide to both the extraordinary and the mundane. In other words, use your values as a basis to live a vision for the future *and* as a focus for daily living. Dream big for your family. You deserve it, and so do they.

A Practice:
Challenging Yourself

In the fast-paced momentum of the times, it helps to have a touchstone or two to be able to reach for in the moment. Concrete expressions of your values you can go to so you don't have to reinvent the wheel each day when it comes to how you choose. Below are some key practical contemplations I have found to be quite powerful in helping to stay aligned with what matters most when it comes to the daily practice of aligning our values with how we use the technologies.

- *In this moment, is a* **text** *being valued over another person?* What is the cost to the relationship?

- *In this moment, is another* **episode** *being valued over a good night's sleep?* What is the cost to mood, health and tomorrow's responsibilities and commitments?

- *In this moment, is* **social media** *being valued over some needed quiet time?* What are the mental, emotional and relational costs?

- *In this moment, is another **Youtube** video being valued over cooking and sharing a homemade meal?* What does this cost the family in terms of cohesion and personal health?

- *In this moment, is a **podcast** being valued over creativity?* Or time to have my own thoughts? What does it cost to be externally stimulated in this way so often?

- *In this moment, is checking **email** being valued over moving my body?* What does it cost my health and well-being?

- *In this moment, is **gaming** being valued over time with the family?* What is the cost to the way it feels to belong to one another?

- *In this moment, is any **screen use** being valued over real life?* What is being missed out on that you cannot get back?

Powerful, value-driven questions practiced throughout the day keep us from rationalizing that we will get back to what matters most to us some other time. It's so easy to not pay attention to what is happening in the moment that we can find ourselves making choices outside our values without even noticing it. If this happens to you, be honest and open with both yourself and your children that right now you're making a choice out of line with what is most important to you, but that you're going to begin the work of closing the gap ASAP. And then, *do it.*

Demonstrate to yourself and to your children that living your values is a process that requires picking ourselves up every single time we fall out of alignment with what is most important to us.

Will it take time to get into a habit of doing things differently? Definitely. *Will there be some griping and resistance?* Absolutely. But I'll tell you firsthand, it's not as ominous as many parents make it out to be. Many parents seem to fear this place. We're so afraid to disappoint. So afraid our children will freak out. Fear not, because the truth is, if your children are never disappointed or upset with the choices you make for them, *you are doing something wrong.* Not getting everything you want and sometimes feeling let down are part of the human experience, and are necessary to build resiliency, patience, tolerance and so much more. We do our children no favors when we sidestep around difficult choices and changes that must be made because we fear their reaction. P.S. If they do seriously flip out, you have undeniable information about the hold an addictive substance has on your child.

Potent Questions

Give yourself your whole life to work on getting clear about what you value, but live as though you only have today. To help you find the balance between generating a sense of urgency, paired with a balanced lifelong commitment to what matters most to you, I offer three simple questions:

- *What do I value?*
- *Am I living those values?*
- *If not, why not?*

Practical Go-To's

- **If you want your values to be the priority in your life, do not make access to the screen technologies quick or easy.** Tuck the screens away. Do not be hasty in fixing or upgrading. Turn the modem off when not in use. Carefully consider how many devices you actually need. Do without every once in a while. Relegate the screens to one place in your home. Remember, you teach your children not only the content of what you value, but as importantly, what it takes and what it looks like to live those values into the world.

- **Set aside time each year to write out and collaborate on your values, goals and dreams for the upcoming year.** Use categories like family, finances, personal, food, health, contribution, home and more. My husband and I have done this each and every year since we got married. We individually come up with our own list, and then collaborate and mesh the two together. It gets written up and posted on our bulletin board in the kitchen. And while I do not always look at it, may even go months without even "thinking" about it, it stands watch over our lives just the same; serving as an ever-present reminder about who we are, and what it is we stand for.

- **Mindfully observe the flow and the routine in your home.** Be as neutral as you can be in your observations. *What do you see?* If you hope to make value-aligned decisions around the technologies in your home, you *must* be willing to see what is *actually* happening. *Not* what you would post on social media. This is especially the case when you come across what is out of alignment with your values.

- **Notice how your mind justifies your choices**. When you are out of alignment with your values, what are the ways that you defend or rationalize what you are doing? In other words, what reasons do you give to yourself or others to explain away why it's okay to violate what you believe in?

Real change comes
from getting to know
the parts of us that
don't want to change.

5
Working With Resistance

"The obstacle is the path."
Zen Expression

My grandfather was a concrete man; literally and metaphorically. He both owned a concrete company, and he lived as if his emotions were set in stone. The entire time I knew him, I never saw him in anything but a suit, a tie and a hat. Even in the summer. I do not remember him laughing, nor was he playful with his grandkids. I don't remember getting hugs from him, or ever touching him. But I do remember being a little afraid of him as he seemed to have zero tolerance for anything outside of his own views. He was the quintessential Irish Catholic stoic who had a rigid sense of what was right and wrong according to the Church. So even though at the end of my grandfather's life, my father told me I had been his favorite, given his distant and cool interactions with me, all I could think was, *"God help the ones who weren't."*

During my early twenties, I worked answering phones in the office at the concrete company. One day I picked up the phone to hear his housekeeper frantically saying to me "Your grandfather, your grandfather…" Based on her alarm and her inability to say what was going on, I thought he must be dead. Or dying. As his house was right next door to the office, I ran over expecting to find him on the floor in the middle of a heart attack or a stroke. Instead, he was sitting in his easy chair, in the piazza as he called it, *bawling his eyes out.*

I stepped across the threshold and into the room, feeling like I had just entered the Twilight Zone. I fully expected the sight of me would make him stop crying. Surely, seeing me would snap him out of this uncharacteristic behavior. Surely, given who he was, he would never, ever, want another human being to witness him in this way. But to my surprise, he kept sobbing. My mind was running wild trying to imagine what this was all about. Could someone have died? Not likely. He had not shed a public tear when his wife of more than fifty years had died. As the housekeeper had already fled the scene, I was left alone with this despondent and grief-stricken man who I no longer recognized as my grandfather.

I quietly sat down in shocked silence.

After a while the sobbing started to dissipate and he began to speak. Even though I was right next to him, it did not feel like he was addressing me. It felt more like he was speaking to himself, and to his own life. He talked about how you live your whole life thinking you're doing the right thing, and that what you believe in is the way to go, but that one day you wake up and realize that it has all been a lie. *All for not.* That you didn't really know what was important. That you had been heading in the wrong direction; making the wrong things important, while missing the really valuable things in life. Now it was too late. Life was nearly over.

When he was done speaking, I told him I loved him and wanted to get to know him better. I told him he had other grandkids who I thought would like to know him better too. I told him he had time and I let him know I was in for this new guy he was trying to tap into. I felt deeply honored and was genuinely happy and inspired to be in the presence of this momentous occasion. I had such a sense of what we could do together with this newfound level of open communication. It was so uplifting for me to see that at any point in time, no matter who you had been for your whole life, no matter how old you were, someone could see "the light" and decide to be different.

The next morning when I went to greet him with the closeness we had ended on, I found myself running head first into a concrete wall! He had completely resurrected his old self; with no insider wink to me, no subtle cue that he would need to wade in slowly, but that we would always be bound by the experience we had shared the day before. No, "I'm scared to be this new guy, and I need help." The opening from the day before was gone. Utterly and completely gone. It left me confused and despondent.

Not only had he closed back up, but now he was even more fortified in some extra and intractable kind of way. The message "keep out" rang resoundingly clear. I only had the heart to make a few more attempts before I stopped trying. A part of me kept hoping one day he might open back up. But it never happened. Not when he had a stroke. And not when he lay dying in a nursing home. The resistance was so complete and so absolutely resolute that it sealed him back into who he had always been. *And then some.* It was as if he had set himself in a concrete mold with no way to reach him. I cannot imagine what it must have taken for him to turn away from the profound knowing he had tapped into on that day. I cannot imagine how afraid and without support he must have felt to turn his back on such a once in a lifetime chance.

The experience left a deep imprint on my young adult mind that carries through to today. It left me with a healthy respect of, plus a lot of grief over, the lengths we will go to reinforce the status quo of who we believe we are and must always be. *No matter what.* To feel we need to hold so tightly to our identities and beliefs, even when it's abundantly clear that what we're doing is hurting us, and those we love.

I bring this story in now because when I look out into our world, and see what is happening to us, including all of the resistance to dealing with what is so out of balance in our lives, I cannot help but to think of the loss and the devastation that our resistance to change is causing us. How it is that despite how much we know and how much we can readily observe, so many of us find it so difficult to change on behalf of our own lives, or the lives of our children.

Standing At A Crossroads

While my focus here is on the devastation that the technologies are wreaking on childhood and on our families, I really could be talking about so many societal issues that are having their way with us. Choices we are making, individually and collectively, that are bringing us further and further away from what is most important in Life. Further away from our values. Further away from real human needs. Further away from the preciousness of the moment. And ultimately, further away from what it means to be human.

It's a most interesting thing in human nature to observe the ways in which we will fight against what would be in our best interest. All of the ways we can know that something *really* must be done, but not be able to get to it for one reason or another. And while it's only natural to want to shy away from what we really need to do when it feels too hard to do, this is exactly the crossroads we are at now: *The place where we can claim what we have been resisting and use it in the service of what we most yearn for.* But in order to be able to do this, we must be willing to invite the resistance in.

Why is that?

Because lasting change comes from more than intellect, willpower, research and the endless stream of information we have come to believe will be what saves us and our children. Instead, real change comes from getting to know the parts of us that don't want to change. The parts that are invested in keeping things the same. The parts that don't have the support they need to allow for change to happen. And the parts that are lacking in a coherent and compelling vision for how to move forward.

There are so many reasons we each have for resisting what needs to be done. There are our histories, our blind spots, our hurts, our pride, our addictions, our ingrained habits, our lacking skill sets, our warped perceptions, our cultural and familial pressures, our lack of support and good role models, and so much more. That's why even when we see the necessity intellectually of making a change, it might not be enough to see us through in the face of the part of us that wants things to stay the same because we can't imagine ourselves any other way. Or because we can't imagine unifying ourselves enough to get up the energy and the stamina we need to overcome the obstacles we will surely encounter. This is nowhere more true than how you live your role as a parent. For if you do not know what drives you, if you are not willing to meet up with the resistance in you to doing things differently, you will be destined to make choices for your child and behave in ways that have nothing to do with what they really need, or for what your lives together calls for.

Reframing Resistance

When we're working with resistance, we have to recognize that it lies outside of our conscious awareness. That's why it can go on for years unchecked. *So how can you change something you're not even aware of?* This has certainly been the domain of all the self-help books, the fields of Psychiatry, Psychology and Behavior Change, as well as all the Eastern awareness practices. That's why I highly recommend you do your own research in this regard and align yourself with some kind of a philosophy and practice that allows you to tap into what you are typically not cognizant of when it comes to who you are and why you do what you do. In a nutshell, find something you believe in that can help you to get to know yourself better. Something that can reveal to you where resistance stops you. Otherwise, you'll stay locked in old, repetitive cycles where nothing actually changes, and where your child is left engaging with the wrong things because you're too resistant to making a change.

But for our purposes here, **what would it be like to get curious about your resistance to a change that needs to be made around technology and your family life?** Some change to be made around what you know isn't working and that brings up discomfort in you. So much so that you avoid doing anything about it. Being with this question will mean challenging the identity you have built for yourself based on a set of assumptions about your role and the role the screens must play in your child's life. For instance, maybe you don't like being wrong and so it's difficult for you to admit you've made a mistake. Maybe there's resistance because to look at something would mean you would need to be around more often and that would be at odds with your work identity and how much of your time your job takes up. Perhaps you believe that without the access your children have now to the technologies they will be friendless, in danger or left behind. And then, of course, there is the unconscious fear we all have that if we change something about who we are and how we are living, those we love and care about won't like us anymore.

Our sense of who we are and how we live does not like to be challenged. It feels too painful. Too vulnerable. More than that, there is an existential component to this where if we are not who we believe ourselves to be, *who are we? And what does that mean about how we have been living up to this point in time?* That's why there will always be a part of us that clings to the old and resists the new. No matter how good or important or hopeful that new might be. I think this is what happened to my grandfather. Because he didn't have a way to context what he was experiencing, he had no way to hold it and work with it. Other than to bring in a complete shutdown around what had been revealed to him.

Resistance As An Ally

Make no mistake about it, resistance is a powerful force indeed; not to be taken lightly, pushed under, denied or forgotten about. That's why I propose we try reframing resistance as a powerful transformative force. One that can launch us in the direction of what we most want and who we most want to be as parents. A perspective we take on where we see resistance as an ally instead of a foe. For instance, we can look to inspiring definitions to help re-think the resistance we experience, ones like: *"Pushing against a source of resistance to achieve strength." "To take a stand." "Something that protects." "The inherent ability of an organism to resist harmful influences."* I don't know about you, but when I read this list, it feels like instructions for how to be a great parent in the times we're living in. Someone who knows how to use the challenges of parenting as a way to strengthen themselves. Someone who knows how to take a stand for childhood. Someone who knows how to protect their young. And someone who knows what to allow in, and what to keep out of their child's life. From this perspective, resistance is not only, most decidedly, *not negative*, it's necessary to encounter and to embrace on our way to making necessary and life-giving adjustments.

As we will discuss many times together in this book, the only way you will be able to make use of what you typically try and get away from is by finding daily and weekly self-observation times that help you connect more fully to who you are and how you make your decisions as a parent. Intentional time on your own that creates unparalleled opportunities to get to know yourself, and why it is you do what you do. Opportunities that will only become available to you when you stop resisting. For as they say, *"What you resist, persists."*

Final Words: A Deeper Examination

For many, many years, I stubbornly clung to a fantasy around what my childhood had been like; portraying it in my mind, and how I spoke of it to others, as having had a kind of idealistic upbringing. Part of my resistance to admitting what it had really been like was because of the stories the rest of the family were telling, and partly because, *I just did not want to know.* I did not want to be that person or have that kind of a family. I did not want to accept what it meant to see that alcoholism had claimed us. I did not want to admit that I had been duped. I was embarrassed. I was grief-stricken. I was enraged. And I was terrified of what would happen if I said that out loud in the presence of other family members.

But somehow, all the resistance to owning up to the truth and all that it was costing me to deny it, got blown wide open when I had kids. Becoming a mother made it impossible for me to go on with the illusion because I could see how agreeing to a lie, while resisting the reality of what had actually happened, was going to cost my children their well-being. That was something I could not bear. I could not do to them what had been done to me. Which is why I say to you now, let your love and your commitment to your children be the force that blows apart any resistance you have to doing what you know needs to be done.

The conscious journey of being someone's parent includes challenging what it is we have always done, thought and believed in. It literally comes with the territory of raising the next generation consciously. *If we can see it that way.* We always have a choice about either stubbornly clinging to what we have always held to be true, or what the culture is telling us, while resisting new information, or we can open ourselves up to a deeper examination of how we are living, and what we are offering to our children. This requires believing that *it is better to know, than to not know.*

An Inquiry:
Resistance Masquerading As Busyness

Busyness and a schedule packed too full can mask all kinds of ills in our lives. For if we never have a moment to be quiet and still, if we never have energy left in reserve, if our attention is continually focused on hitting all of our beats or being fixated on a screen, not only will we miss what is not working, we are guaranteed to have little to give to the changes our lives require as a parent trying to make good choices for our kids. Therefore, ***"Where do you use busyness as a kind of resistance to what needs to be different in your life?"*** Where do you do too much as a way to have nothing left to give? As a way to not have to notice what is really going on? As a way to abdicate taking full responsibility for what is not working with your children?

These are difficult questions to be with. We live in a culture that rewards, *and sometimes even goes as far as demands,* a level of constant going and doing. Those of us who do this "the best" are seen as important and valuable. As seductive as this message is, it is not conducive to a harmonious family life. Nor is it a perspective that will give you any space to consider doing things differently. Your capacity to get control of your own schedule, to limit busyness and to create space for yourself is essential for you to be able to challenge the use of technology in your child's life in a meaningful way. As well as being able to meet the resistance that comes up that you would rather not deal with.

Without clearing your schedule and slowing down to a humane pace, you run the risk of needing to wait for a crisis to incentivize you to change. Those crash phases of life, where we are forced into changing because suddenly the toll that the technologies are taking on our kids hits us square in the face. It may show up as poor school performance because of late nights spent on a cell phone. Or maybe as dangerously low self-esteem brought on by the ravages of social media. Perhaps you'll come face to face with your child's decimated potential being driven by gaming addictions. Or maybe it will be an experience like the parent who told me how her son had cleaned out her bank account to the tune of thousands of dollars to pay for "charms" for a video game.

A Practice:
Letting Resistance Strengthen You

Lest we get too caught up in the weight and density of resistance, what if we took the attitude that any resistance to making changes around the use of technology with our children is to be expected? That it is, in fact, *the very path itself.* When we see it as such, we can learn to work with resistance as a powerful precursor to empowered action. A catalyst that will propel us over the hump if we can learn to see it as an ally.

Therefore, consider inviting your resistance in when it comes to making hard choices around your kids and the devices. Give it a seat at the table. Let it have a voice without needing to shut it up or make it go away. Without needing to do a single thing, other than let it be there, practice for a while saying "Yes" to the fact you wish you were doing something differently, but that you are not. Just for a while, let that be enough as you allow yourself the opportunity to learn from what it is that keeps you from changing.

Fighting against resistance only creates more of it. Watch what happens when you stop resisting the resistance. There will always be a part of you that wants to make changes as a parent trying to do right by their children. *And there will always be a part of you that does not want to change.* This does not make you a bad parent. It makes you human.

What matters most here is you keep going. That the part that wants growth and transformation keeps meeting up with the parts that are in resistance. It is right at this intersection, where what may have seemed insurmountable, will give way into something you never saw coming if you can include the parts of you that resist.

Potent Questions:

Find some time alone where you won't be interrupted. Have paper and pen with you. Consider doing something to make the space you're in feel special, sacred even. Sit down and for a few breaths, just let yourself be. Nothing to do. Nothing to figure out. When you feel settled, ask yourself this question:

"Is there something I know needs to change but that I am resisting for some reason?"

Let the question work on you for a moment while you hold judgment at bay. When you're ready, pick up your pen and begin to write without stopping. Don't worry about grammar, punctation or even if it makes sense. Just open your mind and let it all spill out. And when you have exhausted that answer, pose this question:

What am I going to do about it?

Follow the same process as with the first question. Be on the lookout for resistance. Does it show up in the form of inconvenience? How about overwhelm? Embarrassment? Guilt? What thoughts are you having about your child's potential reaction? Really tap into your feeling state and the emotions that are bound up in this. While the rational, adult mind will line up all of the answers, reasons and justifications, that is not where the resistance lives. It lives in our past, in our histories, in our fears, in our own childhoods. And it reveals itself in our excuses, how busy we keep ourselves and who it is we blame when things aren't going the way we want them to.

Hold these questions lightly without necessarily looking for an answer. Let them work on you, slowly and surely as water works on stone. The more you can notice and release any judgment that comes up around any of this, the more likely you will find your way into some truly life-affirming and elegant understandings of yourself. All of which will form the basis of truly inspired solutions.

Practical Go-To's

- **In a nutshell.** Do Less. Slow down. See tension in your body as a messenger. Say "Yes" when resistance arises and wonder what it has to tell you about being a parent and what you are seeing.

- **Pay attention to the protest.** There is a way we will justify what we know is not quite right for us. See if you can catch yourself doing this. It will show up when you are over-explaining or justifying your choices. Basically, talking too much about something. It will show up when there is mounting evidence you refuse to factor in. It will show up whenever you get defensive.

- **Make it concrete.** Consider a choice around technology and your child that you know needs changing, but have not been able to follow through on. Take out a piece of paper and list out all of the road blocks, fears, hesitations, contradictions and oppositions. And then write "Yes" next to each and every one of them. Doing this does not mean this is where you want to stay. It simply says you recognize that implementing change can be complicated, that something is stopping you, and that if you stop resisting the resistance, something can reveal itself.

Home is where
it all begins.

6
Valuing Your Home Life

"As concerned parents, as concerned human beings,
let us always remember that the best place to start
improving the world is at home."
Annemarie Colbin

When my children would come home from school, I
made it a point to not be in front of the computer or on
the phone. Most days when they arrived I was in the
kitchen doing dishes and prepping for dinner. They would
roll in, plunk down their stuff and the "debriefing" would
begin. In those first few crucial moments, I would get
the full flavor of what their day had been like. They got
to vent or share, while being heard by someone who loved
them. This time together deepened our relationship with
one another, while giving them the support they needed
to deal with all kinds of feelings and experiences that
being a kid brings up.

This was their time to reconnect to home base. It was their time to check in with themselves and meet needs that may have gotten ignored in the rush and pressures of the school day. When we were done reconnecting with each other, they'd get food, go to the bathroom and then wander off to read, play music, create, do homework or zone out. This time of day was all about the space to check in and unwind in a safe and sacred place. With their basic needs tended to, they were better to themselves, others and were in a more balanced position to do homework, chores and any other have-to's. I never needed to tell them that home was important, because we were living it.

I'm aware that not everyone can be at home when their kids get out of school. What I'm proposing here is the recognition that however you do it, you make your home life a priority in real, tangible and kid-friendly ways.

Everything Begins At Home

Home. At its best, home is what nourishes, protects and sustains. Without home, we're lost. That includes all of us—kids and grown-ups alike. Every one of us needs an environment that sustains our lives in healthy and uplifting ways; a place where our truest needs are recognized, honored and met. Like an important conversation, a hug, a reminder, a wholesome snack, a limit, your physical presence. Home is where it all begins for our children and it requires a committed presence there to hold it all together. Otherwise where we live becomes nothing more than a hotel where people come and go.

Home is where our hearts are. It's what holds childhood, and it is what grows our connections to one another. **Our home life must be made a priority if we are to raise happy, healthy and connected children.** Our home is also *the one place* where we can *absolutely* control what comes into our children's lives. So while there will be many, many exposures and experiences we have no control over, *home is not one of those places.* Your home is where you have the power and the authority to draw a clear line. Your home is where you decide what is worthy of your children's innocence, possibility and maturational level.

Home is where everything your child needs to be successful in the world begins; communication skills, self-care, self-worth, team building, lifelong habits, integrity and more. So instead of asking how we can create ways to integrate technology into our children's lives, we should instead be asking how we can make our homes and other living environments responsive to real human needs. Because when the screen-centered life becomes more compelling than the good feelings in our home and the needs of those who live there, we have made the wrong things equate to "home."

The most valuable question then we can ask of our home life is, *"How can we create a space that nourishes and protects the real needs of the people in our family?"* This can be a difficult and strenuous question to ask and live into. To be sure, there are obstacles. We may live far from our families of origin and the neighbors we grew up with, leaving us without a sense of support and continuity. We may be so busy, chronically distracted, exhausted and stressed out that the details of home life can feel like an extra burden in our already overwhelmed lives. And of course, there are all the ways that the devices take away from what nourishes and protects those we love.

But home life is your child's first community, and how we create a home for them matters. That's why there's no overstating the lifelong importance to their health and well-being of this seminal and far-reaching experience. This is where your children get their very first ideas about who they are, how to be in relationship and what to expect from the world. It is where your kids form their habits about how to take care of themselves and how to spend their time. It is where they learn how valued they are and what the most valuable things in life are. What happens in your home matters. *Greatly.*

When No One Is Home

Which is why when we allow the screens to occupy so much of our home life together, we undermine the very fabric of what our kids need, who they are to become and our relationship to them. From the physical to the mental to the emotional to the social to the spiritual; all of who your child is, and can become, is formed, *one way or another*, through the home life you create for them. So while there is a lot you cannot control outside of your own home, this is absolutely the space where what you say goes.

That's why it is so devastating for all of us when home gets the short end of the stick. When our home life is not fully honored, there are dire consequences for our children. In our absences, both physical and emotional, a kind of abdication has occurred where our children have turned to technology to give them what they need in terms of soothing, guidance and connection. *If no one is home, and there is no "home" to come home to, our children will find something else to turn to.* Their need to connect is so compelling that it will find its resolution with whatever substitute is available. No matter how lacking it is. No matter how devoid of true satisfaction. And no matter how barren of real human contact.

The screen technologies, with all of their allure, "promise" and ever-availability, will fill that void if we are not around. A device will stand in your place as parent, mentor and guide if you yourself are MIA, and if your home has become little more than a "docking station." In essence, an iHome. You cannot phone or text this one in. Your children need you in their lives. *In person.* Each and every day. Your children require "someone" or some combination of someone's energies devoted to home, and to the lives of the people living there. *Someone has to put home life at the top of the list.* This may not be popular. This may offend. This may induce guilt. This may bring up resistance. I can speak directly to it all because I have felt it all. And still, it remains so.

This is not about being the CEO of your kids and scheduling them into oblivion. Nor is it about turning yourself into a guilty clown who needs to entertain them all the time. This is never about molding your child into a project to be managed or about creating a better version of you. Most of all, it is never about denying who you are, or about living oppressed. This is about turning our homes into sanctuaries; places where people's truest and most basic needs are honored and respected. Places of refuge that serve to shelter our families against the ravages of over-exposure, over-scheduling and over-consumption.

Figuring out how to create a healthy home is a herculean effort. And yet, it is exactly what our children most need. It is exactly what we all most need. This stands in stark contrast to the over-emphasis on the devices that has left many of us out of touch with our values, our own needs, our children's needs and the value of home life. For some of us to even contemplate exploring home life can generate guilt, shame, competitiveness and defensiveness. But not a single one of us will be served by picking up the burden that our efforts are being judged, or by believing that what we do is never enough. Not one of us will benefit by thinking that the home we create is about meeting some standard of perfection according to another. The truth is, if we spend our energy in these judgmental places, we won't have what we need to create the home we are most meant to create. The one we are all yearning for.

What's Being Lost

One of the greatest, *and most often unrecognized*, downsides of technology in the life of our children are all of the things that go missing. When it comes to our home life, this can look like children being left out of contributing; where too little is asked of them. If not much more is expected of our children than that they be allowed to sit in front of a screen as a centerpiece of their daily existence, they will be relegated to the role of consumers in our homes. This will leave them ill-tempered and unprepared for life. They will lack the skills necessary to live in harmony with others. They will not understand what it takes to run their own lives. And they will squander their time glued to a device instead of creating something of value that gives meaning and purpose to their existence.

Worst of all, if nothing much is expected of them in your home, they will expect very little of themselves. If we do not let them know how much the family needs them, they will not feel needed in the world. Children crave ways they can contribute to their homes and to the ones they love. They need opportunities to experience how to meaningfully contribute to their first and most essential community. That is how important your home life is. This is not something you convey with words, but that you live through your day to day actions.

To make this tangible, look around at your home life. *How do your children spend their time? Are they expected to contribute? How often are their contributions sidestepped or argued over because of their craving for more screen time?* As the parent, you teach your kids what it looks like and takes to be a meaningful member of a community. This means showing them the value, the sacredness even, of home life and of the contributions made to it. By everybody.

Creating A Sanctuary

We all need a place of refuge and protection. This is especially true for children whose innocence must be given shelter, and where anything that violates or diminishes that innocence, is kept out. This stands in sharp contrast to many homes where violence, endless streams of nonsense, graphic images and messages of distorted sexuality are invited guests into our children's lives. This begs the too often unexplored question; *Why are we allowing this?* Why are we letting in the horrific, the lewd, the distorted and the harmful into our very own sanctuaries? And why are we allowing this to happen by our very own hand?

In other areas of their lives, we oversee everything they come in contact with. We pressure teachers into changing grades and offering extensions. We complain to other parents about their child's behavior instead of allowing children to try and work things out on their own. We call upon the principal to accommodate our "special" child. We demand that the jungle gyms be torn down because they are not safe. We do not allow them to run on the hard top and or slide down a mountain of snow because it's too dangerous. *But it is just fine with us that they sit, holed up in their rooms, isolated and un-moving, while they gorge themselves on frightening, aggressive, overwhelming, anti-social, time-wasting and out of their league content and images.* If we are to do right by our children, our homes must serve as a source for what truly nourishes, creates and sustains a healthy human being. We must be dedicated to creating a true oasis that stands as a respite in the midst of a world gone mad.

How do we do this?

We do this by identifying what our core values are, and then sticking to them. *No matter what.* Even in the virtual world. Even in the face of peer pressure or pushback from our own children. We do this by finding the time to get clear on *real* human needs and what age-appropriate experiences are for growing children. And we do this by being present to what is happening in our homes, as opposed to checking out or avoiding what is difficult.

How you create a place of sanctuary is yours to decide and is limited only by your commitment and creativity. For instance, if you can't be physically present to welcome your child home, is there a way you can still support them even in your absence? Some way to check in with them, to be present to them, to ask them about their day? Is there some way you can set up the physical structure of your home to help them focus more on the real world than the virtual one? Is there a life-affirming schedule you can create that gently and firmly holds everyone to their best?

No screen will ever, *ever* do this for your child. This can only happen in the context of a relationship with a caring adult, committed to their child's protection. We must remember, *however it is that we do it,* that how we tend to their needs, how we create the environments they live in, is what they internalize, and how they will do for themselves. Likely for the rest of their lives.

Expanding Our Definition Of Home

In the spirit of a healthy home life, I propose we dismantle the Super Mom (or Dad) stereotype so perfectly depicted in a Mother's Day card I once saw: A gorgeous, voluptuous, sexy Wonder Woman, smile on her face, groceries in one hand and a cell phone in the other, flies through the air. The caption reads, *"Super Heroes have got nothing on you Mom."*

The belief that we're supposed to be sexy, bringing home the bacon and frying it up in the pan, all while we manage the corporate-like scheduling and enrichment programs of our children, is both harmful and untrue. And because home life has been associated with women and the ways we were oppressed, suppressed, demeaned and put down, being the one who tends to home has gotten a bad reputation; often associated with what belittles a woman and holds her back. The stereotype *"a woman's place is in the home,"* limits not only women but makes any man who chooses to fill this role less than, and even an object of suspicion and derision.

I do not know what home life is possible for you and your family, but I do know this: *Someone has to make it a priority.* How you do it, and what it looks like is limited only by your own imagination and ingenuity, and by the ferocity of your commitment to keeping your home people-focused as opposed to machine-focused.

This is not always easy to do in a world dominated by messages from marketers telling us what our families need to buy in order to be okay, look good, be successful and happy. These messages often run counter to our home life because when we buy into the idea that for our children's lives to be worth living, we must be able to buy things for them, lots of things, *especially technological things*, we diminish the real value of home. And we send the message that the gadgets we can afford to give our children are the measure of how well we're doing as parents. Which then, of course, becomes the self-fulfilling prophesy where we now need to be out of the home more often in order to afford all of this.

But when exactly did we trade the sanctity of our homes for flat screens, iPods, smart phones, AI assistants and x-boxes; deluding ourselves into believing these are the makings of a good home? Why is it we have come to believe that inserting a machine into every nook and cranny of our time together makes for a good life? And why do we give the screens such a prominent role in our homes?

When you consider that whatever you allow into your home tells your children what you value most, you take a tremendous risk when you ignore the costs associated with allowing technology to be the most sought after and important focus in your home. Whatever you allow into the life of your family should be a powerful and congruent reflection of your values, and what it is that your children most need. Everything else is a distraction at best, and a violation at worst. That's why it's so important to spend time getting clear about what your definition of home life is for you, and then finding ways to put that into practice.

Final Words: Choosing Happiness

I once had a conversation with another parent who told me of a trip she had taken with her two teenage children and husband, where everyone, per her rule, left their cell phones at home. She spoke of how they sang together on the ride, played games, hung out, talked, made food and hiked together. She fondly spoke of how connected they all felt on this one particular weekend. Upon arriving back home though, everyone went back to business as usual. Phones at the dinner table. Phones pulling people away into their own corners of the house. Phones interrupting in-person conversations. She mused that she should really make some new rules, but that likely given the age of her children they wouldn't go for it. She sighed longingly as she ended the conversation by saying, "We were a much happier family before the cell phones."

If your home is currently overrun with screen life, stop believing this is the only way you can live. Set boundaries based on your values and what you believe is best for your children. Make real human needs and relationships with family members a priority. Put the devices in the position of *always* playing second fiddle to the welfare of your home life. Otherwise, with the technologies being allowed to be everywhere, you're teaching your children that screen life is the most desired part of your home life.

This may be a radical departure from how you've been living. But if you can set the past aside and any pushback you anticipate getting, know this: *If your home life is not working for you, it is not working for anyone else in your family.* Therefore, if you can be brave enough to be with what is not working for you, that discomfort can serve as a catalyst for creating a home you can all feel good about.

An Inquiry:
Real Sacrifice

What is your relationship to sacrifice? Spend some time wondering about how you sacrifice for your children. *What does that look like for you? How does it feel?* The word "sacrifice" is defined as *"the surrender or the destruction of something prized or desirable for the sake of something considered as having a higher or more pressing claim."*

While many parents today would likely say *they are* sacrificing, there also seems to be a lot of confusion around what that actually takes or looks like. There seems to be a feeling among some that the "surrender of something prized" means martyring ourselves, or destroying our careers and the possibility of "the good life." And then there's the way we have confused the need to allow our children to have a "more pressing claim" on us to mean they are entitled to things and activities for which we must always be working to pay for. Or that they get to be the ones in charge. Or that bad behavior is excused away as we work to meet their every whim.

Interestingly enough, in the midst of all of this, the machines have begun to grab the highest and most pressing claim *of all* over many of our lives.

Sacrifice at its highest is about making room for your children in your life, without allowing them to be in charge. *That's what they have a right to.* Their "pressing claim" is to an environment where their truest needs are met. Where they are seen for who they are, and where their childhood is honored and protected. *That's* what they have a right to lay claim to.

A Practice:
Machine Or People Centered

There is so much at stake when it comes to what we are losing when we turn our homes over to machines. Because it has been happening bit by bit, and because it seems like everyone else is doing it, or that this is just how it is or needs to be now, we can be at a loss around how to *feel* the enormity of what is happening in our most cherished of places. Is there something we can turn to then that will offer us a clearer sense of what it is we might be losing?

Yes, by being more present and more awake when we're at home. By paying attention to the look and feel of our lives together with our families. We can do this by regularly wondering, *"Is my home screen-centered or people-centered?"* With this question in mind, and while you keep a lid on the judgment, begin to look around with new eyes at your home life. *What does it feel like to you to be in your home?* What's being given priority? What takes up the most space? What is everyone most interested in?

A screen-centered home puts screens front and center in the physical spaces, giving them a place of prominence; either because of where they're located, or because of how much family time they consume. In a screen-centered home, the devices get in the way of family time, downtime, creativity, sleep, meals and more. On the other hand, a people-centered home values relationships, places of contemplation, creativity and nurturance. It's a home where real human needs like sleep, eating together, building a harmonious home, reading, having fun together and creating are the preferred go-to's.

Use the questions below to create a home that makes sense to you. This is not a one and done exercise, but instead an ongoing kind of check and balance questioning that you do to stay on track with your values and with the sanctity of your family time.

- *"Is my home life working for me?"* Hold this question lightly and let it work on you over time.

- *"What can I do starting today to make my home a sanctuary?"* A place where the allure of the screen pales in comparison to the rich home life I have created.

- *"What problems do the devices create in my home?"* Are the screens in any way interfering with homework, chores, contribution, interactions in real time, friends, pursuing personal interests, outdoor time, creativity, sleep, play, quiet time, people's moods, mealtimes or the peace and sanctity of my home?

- *What is one small step I can take to put the screens out of the sight, minds and hearts of my family in an effort to make more room for a home that truly provides what everyone is really needing?* In other words, out of sight, out of mind.

Begin by making changes where it's easiest. Pick one area to work on and build from there. This could mean setting limits about when, where and how the devices are being used in your home. Maybe it means holding off buying kids their first cellphone or giving them access to social media. Maybe it means putting your own devices to the side while you are at home with your kids.

Practical Go-To's

Home is an external place and an internal experience. Something as basic as how you have your home set up, and what is in it creates the fundamental structure of your family's life. Look at the overall flow, rhythm and placement of things in your home. What does it *feel* like to be there? Relaxing? Chaotic? Nourishing? Noisy? Distracting? Grounding? Below are some things to consider on your way to making your home sacred for you and your family.

- **Quiet, stillness and reflection matter in your home.** All humans need this to be well.

- **At its best, your home life is a reflection of your deepest values.** Is what you value front and center in your home?

- **Make technology a conscious choice in your home.** When screen time is a decision you are making, does your choice reflect your values and the developmental needs of your child?

- **Look at your physical environment.** What technologies do you own? Where and how are they positioned throughout the house? The items you give prominence to in your home tells your children *everything* about what you value most.

- **Keep your kitchen a nourishing space.** There is a reason why at any gathering, no matter how crowded or inconvenient, the kitchen is where people gravitate to. Be very protective and conscientious about keeping screen time from interfering with your family's ability to gather together and be nourished. This is your heart space. Therefore, *do not allow any technology at the table.* Allowing your child to zone out in front of a screen while they are eating is a very destructive and difficult habit to break. While the screens may keep your child quiet and controlled, they are being trained to live disconnected from the signals of their bodies. Keeping technology away from the dinner table not only helps your child be more connected to their bodies, they will be more connected to you. Table talk is how our children learn about everything. Around your dinner table, they are learning language, turn-taking, your mores, their own voice and the customs of your family. *Do not miss this time with your children.* You will hear about what is on their minds and in their hearts. And you will build a relationship with them that stands at the very center of what home means to them.

- **Protect the sanctity of the bedroom.** If your child has technology in the bedroom, you can count on them getting into things you would *never* approve of. It puts your child at risk for exposure to content that far exceeds their ability to process it, and keeps them up late into the night. It is far too easy as a parent to be lulled into the peace and quiet we are getting while they are being sucked into the virtual world. Nothing, and I repeat, *nothing* good is happening late at night when your child is left all alone and unattended with a screen. When we leave our children all alone, with nobody monitoring their use and what they are being exposed to, we open them up to the wrong things. Lastly, it has been well documented that sleep deprivation results in lower grades, an increase in accidents, poor health, weight gain, moodiness, disease, stress and an increase in depression.

- **Say "No" to violence in your home.** Why are we allowing innocent children to entertain themselves on harm? If you find yourself justifying this one, *look more deeply.*

- **Create screen-free spaces.** Work to establish places in your home that encourage gathering, stillness and creativity free from the demands of the machines. If a screen is prominently displayed, or a device is open, the temptation is just too strong, and will serve to undermine reading, talking, zoning out, playing games and more. All of these activities and ways of being are absolutely essential to your child's unfolding development and your relationship to them.

- **Turn off the devices.** A simple, elegant and effective way to keep the screens in their place is to refrain from leaving them on all the time. Be goal-directed when you turn on a device. In other words, do what you have to do, *and then turn it off.* Never allow the machines to be background noise or always available.

- **Eliminate any and all screen use that gets in the way of your family time together.** Nothing more needs to be said here.

Every experience children have contributes to who they are to become.

7
Tuning Into What
Kids Really Need

*"To put it simply, childhood is our species' evolutionary edge.
Childhood takes time. And many children are simply not being
given the time to be children."*
Healthy Children, Healthy Planet

I was once proudly shown a video of a nine-month-old
who had "the greatest laugh ever." For the first few seconds
of the video the baby was engaged and giggling as her
mom tickled her. However, in no time at all, the baby
went eerily blank. She stopped laughing. There was not
even a hint of a smile left on her face. She had broken
eye contact with the adults and her expression had turned
to stone. It was painful to watch the rapid transformation
of her going from full engagement, to being completely
shut down.

What was even worse was witnessing how this shift went
unnoticed by the grown-ups. Though her face had gone

expressionless, though she had turned her head away from the grown-up tickling her and though her little body had gone rigid, she continued to be mercilessly tickled and filmed, despite the fact that every part of her had checked out. I had the strong sense this was not the first time this baby had been through this.

The tickler and the videographer failed to notice the cascade of non-verbal cues of distress this baby sent them because they were too caught up in capturing this moment for others to see. They were too immersed in letting the technologies be the priority to notice all the non-verbal cues this baby was sending—begging for them to stop. They didn't get any of this because they were too disconnected from the fact that what a grown-up with a machine might find awesome, would be intensely overwhelming for a baby.

Disconnected from the moment and from the real needs of this child, the adults ignored and overrode multiple signals this little one was sending. If she could have spoken, it would likely have sounded like, "I've had enough. I'm shutting down now because I'm so overwhelmed. I wish you would stop." It was excruciating to watch, and even more excruciating to extrapolate out what moments like this do to a developing human being. A litany of events strung together that on their own may not seem like much, but that when taken together begin to create a life where children must learn to shut down in order to survive the world we have thrust upon them before they are ready for it.

Without realizing it, the adults in this scene gave this child the message that preening for the camera is more important than your own comfort—teaching her to become "comfortable" with her instincts being overridden. Instead of connecting with her, they placed a machine in between themselves and this baby. Can you imagine how this might play out for this child in the years to come in regard to social media or with sexting or with predatory encounters? Extrapolating out for all of the younger generations past, present and future, what will it do to them to regularly have their needs ignored and overridden in the service of something non-human? Will they go on to do the same to themselves? Will they go on to allow others to do the same to them?

Letting Children Be Children

Every single experience our children have is contributing to who they are to become—growing their sense of themselves and their view of the world. Like a tapestry being woven, thread by thread, each and every experience adds to the creation of the whole of them. What this means for us as the gatekeeper of childhood is that we seriously evaluate the experiences we allow into their lives. Looking not through the lens of a grown-up, but through the lens of how a child might be receiving these experiences.

Consider this. In the beginning, your child's only need was you, along with basic care, love and protection. Your child came into this world open and innocent, with no needs other than the most basic for food, sleep, protection, warmth, connection, touch and age-appropriate experiences. By meeting these basic and life-giving necessities, you teach your children they have a place in the world. That there are those they can count on. That there is an order of importance when it comes to how to live a life. This is as basic as food. Shelter. A regular schedule. It is our closeness to them. It is how we tend to their most basic human needs. It is how we protect them from what might overwhelm their non-existent capacity to be with the dangers and harshness of the world. Initially, it is all very physically based. But it is out of this physical basis that the foundation is laid for emotional, mental, social and spiritual health and well-being.

In other words, what we do for them early on, impacts everything that follows when it comes to the totality of who they are and who they will be.

Suffice to say, you do not need to get trained or go back to school to become an expert in this. Instead, it's about learning to make a whole-hearted attempt to figure out what your children really need as they are growing. This understanding is born of your capacity to be present, to align with what is most important to you, and to be brave enough to ask the deeper questions about what is happening with your children in regard to the technologies.

This is not a call for infantilization or raising entitled children. It is not about bubble wrapping them and feeding them with a steady diet of things to be afraid of. Instead, this is about taking up our role as their guardian; despite what the culture is pushing for. And it is to work to get a clear picture of what the real developmental needs of our children are, and how they serve as *the lifelong foundation* for all that they are, and all that they will be. Anything that interrupts these processes is the enemy of your child's childhood.

This includes breaks in conversation with you because you got a text, sleepless nights because of being up late on a device, disruption in play and time outside because the screens are more interesting. Various disciplines like psychology, medicine and child development list the ills that befall children whose growth is interrupted. We know it in the child who does not get the nutrients they need to grow a healthy body, and who experiences a lifetime of illness because of it. We see it in the child who is neglected or abused in ways that break their spirit, and warp their emotions, leaving them unable to connect with others or to trust themselves. And we have witnessed it firsthand in the children who are subjected to harmful environmental toxins in utero or at a young age, and who suffer widespread and systemic mental and emotional damage because of it.

A Common Sense Tutorial

Understanding what children need at different ages is an enormous topic. There are many perspectives from various schools of psychological and developmental thought, as well as familial ideas, spiritual traditions, and cultural norms regarding what children need to grow. For the purposes of our exploration here, I'm offering a big picture approach; one based in common sense and backed by your own direct observation. One not focused specifically on particular stages of development, but instead, on universal principles, concepts and understandings of what supports healthy growth.

Growth is a layering process—sometimes slow to reveal or take effect, often beneath the surface, but happening just the same. The full and healthy expression of your child's development is a decades-long journey and culminates in what they have been given, as well as what they have missed out on. Immediate cause and effect correlations between what our children are exposed to and the outcomes on their growth are not always obvious.

Below are simple, basic concepts I read about or discovered personally you could use when trying to figure out your child and what they need. And if you're really at a loss, get some help from sources who have no agenda other than what's best for kids.

- **Development is cumulative.**

- **Children must be allowed to be *every age* they are for healthy lifelong development to occur.**

- **There is a natural progression and unfolding in development that cannot be forced, coerced or deprived without consequence.**

- **Different ages and stages of development have critical and sensitive time periods that if missed or tampered with create impairment.**

- **Unmet developmental needs have drives that continue to persist.**

- **Children are deeply sensitive.**

- **Before our children can be independent, their dependency needs must be satisfied.**

- **If it is not working for your child at the age and stage they are at, it will not be working for them at a later time.**

- **For every hour spent in front of a screen, there is the risk that something is not happening during crucial windows of your child's development.**

Challenging The Abnormal

We have so thoroughly come to believe that without the screens our children will be left behind. That they will have no friends. That they will be in danger. *But what if the opposite were true?* What if, despite the current belief that we need to be constantly managing and organizing them through the devices, our children's innate and natural curiosity, creativity and connectivity are what most needs our time and attention? What if we are un-teaching them their most important instincts and impulses by exposing them too early and too often through too much technology? *What if we are robbing them of their integrity, character development, self-esteem, intuition, social skills, confidence and more by our overemphasis on technology in childhood?*

No child is born with an inherent need for screen time. No instinctual need to post, text or tweet. No innate drive to obsessively carry around a hand-held device. We have built this into them. We have allowed the tech companies and other interests to separate us from what we, as mammals, know deep down inside is necessary for the health of our young. The pace of the Information Age *is not* the pace of childhood. If we were really being honest, it is not the pace for any *living being*. We have made the importance and the speed of the machines our new "normal"–not recognizing in the whirlwind of it all, that busyness, speed and information overload are the enemies of childhood.

No child comes into this world needing to do more and more and at faster and faster rates. Speed and convenience, while the domain of the technologies, are *never* the criteria by which to measure what it is our children require. Raised with too much, too soon, too fast and too often, the necessary, organic evolution of childhood is thwarted. Healthy development cannot be trifled with, without grave consequence. The subtlety, nuance, direction, sequencing and simplicity of our children's growth is not haphazard. It is not random. *But it is sensitive.*

Wouldn't it be prudent to more fully understand what you're actually agreeing to? To think long-term before you say yes? To push the pause button long enough to gain an accurate assessment of the technologies impact on every single level of their development? To challenge any notion or agenda that is in conflict with supporting healthy childhood? ***Wouldn't it be visionary of us all to look all the way down the road, beyond our children's childhood to be on the lookout for any and all unintended consequences and harms?***

A father once told me he felt the decision to give his 6th grader a cell phone was the equivalent of her losing her virginity. Despite the no-going-back nature of this — he still said *"Yes."*

Children Are Born Wise

Here's the good news. Our children are naturals when it comes to developing. They know how to move when they need to move, sleep when they need to sleep, eat when they need to eat and be with those they most need to be with. If our children are given the honoring and the protection they need, it supports them in doing what every human being knows how to do; access the wisdom they were born with that enables them to move towards what satisfies their most important needs.

If you can begin to check in with your own observations and what it is you value most, you begin to see that your child's development occurs in its own exquisite way; according to internal clocks and rhythms that function best when supported by appropriate nourishment from you and the way you set up their life. This is what helps to melt away all of the hype, the external pressures, the confusions and the brainwashing we are all subjected to. All of the things that can pull us off course as our child's gatekeeper.

Check it out for yourself. Can you see that each stage of your children's growth is important unto itself, *and* because of the ways that it serves as a stepping stone for everything that comes after it? If you look closely, you can see it in how the babbling of your baby is wisdom in action and is the basis for language and interpersonal connection.

If that same baby is met by a screen instead of a loving person in real time, communication and relational intelligence will be compromised at a fundamental level.

Every single experience your child has grows them. Informs them. Wires their brain and their physiology. What you expose them to sets their expectations, needs, wants and desires. Our kids are pure wise potential just waiting for the opportunity to reveal this day by day. Best of all, you do not need to make this happen. Instead, you need to support it. You do this by being present, by listening deeply and by observing them. This is what will help you follow their developmental lead. If this makes sense to you, *what would it be like to sit back more, trust more, observe more, interfere less, buy less and impose the screens less, all while allowing Nature to take its course more naturally?*

It's important to point out that following their lead does not equal leaving it all up to them, or expecting them to be the one in charge. Instead, it means being guided by where they are at; recognizing who it is that stands before you, while paying attention to their signs and signals. All while remaining steadfastly as the one in charge.

Play

I once heard that play is the work of children. But in our fast-paced technological times, we ignore this essential building block. We trade open-ended time in childhood with all of its unlimited possibilities for a far too long list of "educational" apps, enrichment programs, play dates, organized sports, forced music lessons and more. All of this being done in an attempt to "advance" and prepare our children.

We, as the over-scheduled and over-burdened adults in their lives have come to believe that if our children are busy, have early exposure to computers, along with extracurriculars of all sorts, that as parents, we are doing our job. We have come to believe that the never-ending treadmill we are on, the anxiety generated by trying to keep up, and the competition we feel around other parents and what kid is doing what, is part of raising a healthy family now. That this is how we give our children all the "advantages" they need.

When I would speak with friends who were elementary school teachers, what I heard most often was that kids had forgotten how to play, and that their ability to create from their own imagination was noticeably and alarmingly, *missing*. This is nothing short of devastating. When these same teachers would ban all talk or school projects based on movies, TV shows or video games, the children could not come up with a single idea. They were absolutely stumped as to what they should write about when they could not reference characters and themes that had come out of a screen.

For our children to be without imagination and play is the equivalent of imagining birds without wings. *This is not natural. Creativity and play is the very heart, soul and essence of childhood.* To watch it go missing is the equivalent of watching a species go extinct. It is heartbreaking and soul crushing to witness.

Children do not require external devices to bring their imagination alive. The current trend of turning them to a screen at earlier and earlier ages is systematically stealing their originality, inspiration and the delight that comes out of creating from within. The screens are leaving our children chronically, perpetually and externally entertained and over-stimulated. This has turned them into performers and people-pleasers for their followers instead of playing and engaging together with friends in innocent childish pursuits. It has left them searching for apps that make their work, their games, their explorations, their art and their imagination for them, as opposed to bringing into the world what it is that is within them.

Boredom

Right alongside the loss of play is its companion. Boredom. One of the greatest mistakes modern day parents make is ensuring that their children are *never bored.* We have come to equate boredom with so many things. We worry it means we are not doing enough. We fear our children will be left behind if they are not constantly engaged at all moments, and from the earliest of ages. We believe that to keep them busy means we are doing our job.

One of the best gifts you can ever give your child is the space to be bored. Do not allow every ounce of their time to be filled. Do not let them stuff their days full of screen preoccupations and obsessions. To grow soundly into adulthood, your children *must* know boredom in their lives. *Regularly.* It is the yellow brick road to creativity, perseverance, self-initiative and so much more. It requires, though, you being courageous enough to allow for open space in their life. In other words, *stop filling the empty times with a screen.* As a college professor, I heard from too many college students, far too often, of the ways they would waste away hours each and every day in front of a screen simply because they did not know what to do with themselves. They did not know how to be with themselves when nothing was entertaining, structuring and stimulating them. They did not know how to be alone and see that as an opportunity. And they would often describe life without a screen as "empty."

Right about now, you might be thinking, *"But what will my kids do without a device?"* It's important to remember that until the recent decades, generation after generation grew up without the screens, and found more than enough to do. As a matter of fact, the originators of the first screen technologies never grew up with any of the devices they would go on to create. *What was it then that allowed them to be so inventive?* Out-of-the-box thinking, lots of open space to imagine, time spent in boredom, play and lots more like it that can only come out of a child being allowed to be a child.

Let yourself take a big leap of faith here; trust that what your child needs in this department is built in. Step back. Have faith. Give space. Don't fix. Don't do for. And if you've been structuring their time for them or allowing the screens to do it for them, *there will be an adjustment period.* Count on it. While it can feel *extremely* challenging initially to not cave into their demands or slip back into old ways of being, learn to hold your ground while you hold both yourself and them in the knowledge that boredom is good. Then give them and yourself enough time and space for them to settle into what comes out of them naturally when the screens are not the dominant force in their life.

You Already Know The Answer

You already have within you everything you need to observe what you are seeing and to feel what you are feeling about what is happening with your children. Every answer you need lies somewhere inside. Trust yourself. You do not need to be a child development expert to know what to do when it comes to the screen technologies and your child. Push aside the hype, the doubts and the fears. You already have everything you need to know about what kids need to develop in a healthy way. It's basic. It's the same as it's always been. They need love, consistency and protection. They need sleep and whole, clean food. They need lots of time to play. They need to be outside. And they need to be connected to people who care about them and who spend time with them. Most of all, *they need you, a sane life and a sacred home.*

Spend more time looking at your kids. ***Where do you think the use of technology in your child's life flies in the face of their inherent wisdom to develop?*** Pay attention. It's everywhere when you know what to look for. You can see it in the distortions in our young people's posture and body language. It is in the way they orient to and crave machines over people. It is in their lack of attention, eye contact, creativity and the ability to be alone comfortably. It is in the way they would rather text than talk. It is in their fears, anxieties and behavioral outbursts. It is in the way they remain motionless, glued and transfixed by a screen; despite the basic and natural imperative to move. You can see it when the deep necessity of face to face time with children of all ages and caregivers in real time is regularly interrupted by screen use. It is evident when we put babies and young children in front of a screen to keep them quiet and occupied despite the collective wisdom that tells us that mobility and exploration in young children is essential. You can observe it when the crucial and sensitive work in adolescence of developing an independent sense of self along with social skills, is daily distorted through unlimited and un-monitored access to cell phones and social media.

No matter how you cut it, as a parent, you *must weigh in* on this. As a matter of fact, someone should have checked in with us first before rolling out the technologies to our children. That level of accountability, foresight and protection of the vulnerable among us would have been the sign of a world that *really* took care of its young. Since that did not happen, it is up to you to take full responsibility for your family. Up to you to tap into what you already know. Forget about what you have been told. Forget about what the school says. Forget about what your neighbors are doing. Forget about what your pediatrician says. If your child would rather be in front of a screen than with people, if your child is exhausted because of late nights up with their devices, if they would rather text than talk, if they are being entertained by violence, if they cannot be alone, if they are anxious, if they cannot fall asleep on their own, if they tantrum when the screens are taken away, if they live more in the virtual world than the real world, if they spend more time desperately seeking "likes" than actually living their lives, *YOU ALREADY HAVE YOUR ANSWER.*

Now what?

What You Can Expect

When you allow your children time for a childhood and an adolescence free of excessive screen influence, you can look forward to children who know how to entertain themselves and have the ability to turn boredom into something valuable. You can count on children who can be alone with themselves and enjoy the company they keep. You can look forward to way less nagging and arguments over homework and chores because of them being lost in a virtual reality. Less friction between you and them allows for other possibilities in your home. Like the deepening of your connection to them. Like a more peaceful feeling in your home.

You can also look forward to kids who get the sleep they need, allowing them to be healthier, easier to get along with and more successful in school. You can count on children who know that what matters most cannot be bought or plugged into. You can expect kids who naturally make eye contact, are not afraid to talk on the phone or put themselves out there in new or challenging social situations. You can expect to be around children who are not anxious or depressed because of screen over-stimulation. You can expect to be with children who love to read, play music, hang out and converse, along with whatever else is theirs to uniquely tune into. You can expect a deep and inner resourcefulness they call their own. You can also count on kids who know how to ground themselves through the time they spend with their family. Best of all, you can expect to be in relationship with individuals who know how to think for themselves and who value connection. This is the short list. The very, *very* short list.

Final Words: Restoring Childhood

Once when my husband and I were doing the rare thing of going out to dinner, just the two of us, my daughter, upon learning she would have the house to herself, opted to stay home. Why would a 17-year old want to stay in a home that had no cellphone, TV, Ipad, Facebook, friends or non-permission based access to a computer?

So she could be on her own. *That's why.* Maybe she would play her guitar or sing. Maybe she would work on an art project, call a friend, read, putz around or cook. Who knows? She might even be bored. But at that point in her life she had weathered enough boredom and open space to not only know its value, but to actively seek out its reward.

The truth is, when our children are truly living, that is, playing, resting, contributing, sleeping, learning, creating, sharing meals and interacting with others, there is very little time left over for screen life. That's why the heart of this conversation we're having is about focusing on what is already inside the life of your child, and what you can do to support that.

Finally, there is no guarantee when it comes to raising children. No perfect formula to make everything turn out the way we want it to. No matter what we do, things will happen, and our children will go on to live their own lives (hopefully) as they see fit. Therefore, the choice to honor the preciousness of our children's childhood does not offer any certainty or guarantee. But that is not why we do what we do. We do what we do because it is our job to protect them. We do it because that is why we are here.

An Inquiry:
Back To Basics

Try a thought experiment where you imagine back to times before there were the technologies we have now. *During those times, what do you imagine the adults would say children needed to be healthy and connected? What were the most important things children had and did to grow into healthy and resilient adults?* In this thought experiment, you might also imagine what it is on the most basic of survival levels, that your child could absolutely not live without. You might even pretend to have a conversation with a distant and wise relative who could help you see through the hype and the pressures around technology and your children. Perspectives that might help you see that despite the presence of cell phones and lap tops, human biology and psychology *has not changed.*

What our children really need was beautifully highlighted by a student of mine once who reported that his phone had broken, and that he had been without it for an entire day. *The longest he had gone in his ten year relationship with his device.* When he told this to the class, I mocked an exaggerated gasp. *"A whole day without your phone?!! That must have been awful."* But it wasn't. When I asked him what it had been like, he said "FREEING!" Interestingly enough, this is the same student who, earlier in the semester, had reported his concern at discovering that even when he had no missed call, text or notification, he would obsessively find himself fiddling with his phone. Unable to stop and put it down. He could not explain the compulsion, but it concerned him. *A lot.*

As you imagine what it is your child truly needs, let your mind turn towards what is non-negotiable in Life, as opposed to the modern day "musts," and you might just imagine your way into the greatest freedom they could ask for.

A Practice:
Look At Your Kids

The screens do not smile or offer a hug. They cannot set an appropriate limit. They cannot guide your children to love themselves or convey how much they matter. They will never teach them how to self-regulate or read an emotional cue from another. They will not help your child eat well or get the sleep they need. They will never help them engage in healthy movement or habits. They will not mitigate the roots of loneliness, boredom or temper tantrums. They are not the source of creativity. And they will never, *ever*, be an adequate substitute for you or friends in real time.

With this in mind, spend some time mindfully observing your children. Pay attention to what happens as they engage with a screen. *REALLY* look at them. *What do they look like to you?* How is their body positioned? What do you see or imagine is happening inside their growing mind? What is their mood like before, during and after? How do they respond when you set a limit regarding screen time? How well do they connect with others in real life? Are they more comfortable in the virtual world? Is being in front of a screen what interests them more than anything else?

Specifically, be on the lookout for *what is not happening*. For instance, when they are in front of a screen, what does not happen for them regarding play, personal interests, sleep, time with you, creativity, downtime, chores, exploration and so forth? *The regular absences that are occurring in our children's lives are perhaps more telling than anything else about the impact the devices are having on them.*

Potent Questions

No child comes into the world needing a screen to be fulfilled, connected or happy. The questions below can serve as powerful check-ins to help you be on the lookout for what is being replaced in your child's childhood that they cannot afford to miss out on.

- *What does it mean if the biggest influence in your child's life comes out of a machine?*

- *Without the electronics, what would your child naturally gravitate to?*

- *When have you seen your child experience true happiness?*

- *What does it mean for your kids if they believe their value is based on "likes?"*

- *When you first had your child, was there a feeling you had about what you wanted to give to them or the kind of world you wanted to create for them?*

While we could argue that modern life requires certain technological things of us now, we must endeavor to remember that the true necessities of childhood are love, friendship, protection, clean food and water, sleep, time to play, a sane and humane pace, a safe environment, human connection and a right to innocence. Below are some ways to ensure your children have the time, the space and the protection they need to grow in healthy ways.

- **Do not start any habit you do not want to maintain.** Avoid using the digital world as a pacifier.

- **Out of sight. Out of mind.** Do not allow the technologies to be so readily available.

- **Keep electronics out of their play.** Period. Whether on their own or with other kids.

- **Dedicate a bin to childhood.** Stock it with ingredients for their own creations.

- **Let your children be bored.** Boredom is the road to creativity and self-empowerment.

- **Stay vigilant to machine themes.** If you hear your child mimicking screen life, they are being robbed of their originality.

- **Your children need to be outside.** Every single day, and not organized by you.

- **Don't push their days.** Reduce or eliminate screen exposure as often as you can and for as long as you can. Give them the chance to be children.

- **Before you say "Yes."** Ask yourself, "Is this choice age-appropriate?"

- **Know what motivates your decisions.** *Why are you making the choices that you do?*

- **The leading edge.** Let their developing needs inform you. Notice without assuming.

- **Filling the void.** Without your presence, the screens will fill the space that is yours to fill.

- **Look through the lens of a lifetime.** What you choose for them today, they will choose for themselves tomorrow.

- **Avoid the "seamless" life.** Let there be difficulties, boredom and inconvenience. This is what builds character.

- **Say YES! to childhood.** YES! to secure attachments with you. YES! to creativity. YES! to innocence. YES! to a strong and healthy sense of self. YES! to critical thinking. YES! to strong and satisfying connections with others. YES! to physical health and play. Yes! to unstructured time.

Protecting our children and projecting irrational fears onto them is not the same thing.

8
Challenging Your Fears

"Our fears are more numerous than our dangers,
and we suffer more in our imagination than in reality."
Seneca

When my daughter was in her sophomore year of high school, I dropped her off at The Putney School in Vermont for a three week internship working on their dairy farm. I left her with a little money and some food to fill in for what she couldn't get in the dining hall. That was it. No cell phone. No laptop.

As I got into my car to leave, I unexpectedly burst out crying. It took me some of the ride home to catch up with the emotions that had come over me. It wasn't because I was afraid or couldn't bear to be without her. Instead, I was moved to tears at the thought that my sixteen year old was getting a chance to be on her own. I felt so excited for her. And for us. *Why?* Because I was confident not only in her own abilities but also in the strength of the bond between us.

In that moment, I could really see, perhaps for the first time, what the structure of our home life had provided for her. A structure that had given her opportunities to be independent and resourceful. This was what allowed me to let her go for the longest time we had ever been apart. Without needing to check on her. Without needing to satisfy or indulge my own concerns or curiosities. Without needing to insert myself daily into her experience. Without needing to impose fears on her about what would happen if we were not in constant contact.

During her time away there were a couple of letters, but that was it. For three weeks, there were no texts, calls or emails. I had the head of dorm's phone number should I need to be in touch, and there was a house phone in the common area should she feel the need to contact us. We did receive one phone call from her the night before I was to pick her up asking if she could stay until the end of the weekend. What a great call that was to receive. To hear that she was doing so well being away, that she wanted more time.

Throughout her time away, there was no anxiety about her because I knew that what she needed was inside of her, because I have a deep and abiding trust in Life, because she had been "in training" for this moment for years, and because our relationship was strong and stable enough to not just withstand the time apart, but to be strengthened and enriched by it.

I recognize in this day and age, a story like this might seem shocking. Or unsafe. Maybe some would say irresponsible and negligent to allow an adolescent to be away without a cell phone. Maybe it might serve to some as proof I didn't care about her. Or that I was naive. But it was none of that. It was instead a rite of passage. Necessary for her development. Supported and deeply honored by my lack of involvement. All of which came together to give my daughter a chance to spread her wings all on her own to see what it was like to fly without us.

A Culture Of Fear Is Born

My children were two and four on 9/11. On that day I was with people who were trying to get in touch with friends from New York, not knowing if they were okay or not. My brother was out of contact traveling along the east coast, maybe in New York City, maybe not. Many of us did not know where friends and family were, and whether or not they were alive. It was terrifying. The illusion we Americans held about having a kind of protective immunity available on our own soil was shattered. That one day alone changed everything for us—rippling out in ways we never could have imagined.

A new culture of fear was born on that day. With it came the idea that it was dangerous to be out of touch with the people in our lives. The new culture of fear said, *"This could happen to you. You might never see your loved one again."* At the same time this devastating message was taking hold, technological advancements promising instant and continuous connection were exponentially exploding into our everyday lives in the form of cell phones. The phones quickly became the symbol of safety, certainty, control and security when it came to us and others. The guarantee of staying in touch with loved ones, *always and from anywhere*, arrived just when we were at our most vulnerable. Just when our fears around disconnection and loss were at their highest. The promise of never, *ever*, being "out of touch" became the new anthem. Our children were the first monkeys into space on this one.

All of this would be so poignantly represented to me over the years to come through the college classes I was teaching. *"What if something happens?"* was a question I would be regularly asked whenever my college students would hear that neither myself nor my children had cell phones. Whenever it came up, I would reply, *"Something is going to happen. Life is going to happen."* This was never the answer they were expecting. And it certainly was not what they wanted to hear. It was too edgy. Too raw. Too real. And the devices were far too seductive in their ability to convince us all we would always be safe. *Which is why so few of us ever questioned their place in our lives.*

It's so easy to be afraid these days. It has become a modern day habit. It's socially supported. *Expected even.* One could argue that it has become an addiction of sorts. Whether obsessing on our news feeds that focus on what bleeds, constantly talking about all the things we are afraid of now or entertaining ourselves on the violent and the gory, there is seemingly no end to how what is disturbing and frightening has become the backdrop of our lives. All of this goes on to cement in our minds how terrifying and dangerous the world is; justifying why we must all carry a machine around in our pockets and purses. We have been convinced we need it, and that our children need it, in order to be safe. Which is why so few of us could ever imagine stepping back from all of this. Fear, it seems, shuts off our capacity to critically think.

But what if it was just the opposite? ***What if taking in so much fear via the screens scrambles our natural ability to discern real from false dangers?*** And what if the belief that a cell phone is what keeps you and your children safe, has an enormous unrecognized and unchallenged downside?

In The Grips Of Fear

Fear is a most interesting phenomenon. It is a basic and elemental aspect of our innate survival system; serving a non-negotiable role in the life of any mammal. An undeniable, built-in, unconscious force that in the face of *real* and immediate danger, acts instantaneously and unconsciously to do whatever it takes to keep us alive. The problem comes in for us when the modern day mind conjures up fears where there are none. Of course, this is also being amplified by corporations who know all too well *exactly* how to hijack this part of the brain; pushing our buttons in the service of what they want us to do. And because it just feels too dangerous to challenge whether our fears are real or imagined, *we don't.* Partly out of habit, and partly because our survival system can't tolerate taking a chance when it comes to what it sees as life and death. Even if it's made-up.

Ironically enough, our children often go unprotected on many levels because of *the very thing* we have purchased to keep them safe. For instance, they drive distracted—directly putting themselves and others in harms way. They entertain themselves on the gruesome and the explosively sadistic and violent—leaving them stressed, overwhelmed and afraid. They gorge on information that focuses on the extremes, and they choose cell phone interactions with others that exploit their innocence through practices like sexting.

Because their bodies do not seem to be in imminent danger, we fail to recognize that the images and the information they ingest generates a fear-based perspective that is not representative of reality. Flooded with stress, fear and anxiety, their poor little bodies, minds and souls deteriorate. Simultaneously, because they live in a fantasy world of dangers, they are woefully disconnected from, and unprepared for, the true realities of life because there is no gaining competency when *the danger is not real.* In other words, there is no way for them to address what is happening, and therefore, no way for them to develop skills they could use in the future *because what is happening is not real.*

And because they have a device in their possession, they believe they are equipped to meet life's challenges when, in fact, *they are not.* Their over-reliance on the screens puts them in the position of not being aware of their surroundings because their attention is so immersed in a machine, and because they have bestowed an omnipotent, god-like status to the devices; believing their cell phones possess capacities to save them and to problem-solve real world situations that only a human brain is capable of. Our children are grossly under prepared, while believing they are more prepared than they are. This is a dangerous and destructive combination.

The Worry Game

Real biologically-induced fear responses are not the same thing as worrying. Worry is manufactured fear. It is something we make up. ***Real fear, on the other hand, is a survival response to real danger.*** We are mistaking being a good parent with how afraid we are, and how much we worry. We are under the mistaken assumption that we can address our worries by making choices that seem to control the source of our worries; like when we believe giving our children a cell phone to know where they are at all times will keep them safe.

The absolute truth is though, *there are no guarantees* when it comes to the safety of our children. The unspoken belief that we will all be safe as long as we are constantly connected to each other via our phones has come to replace the reality that *Life offers no such guarantees*, and that our relationships are only as good as the real time and the effort we put into them. But this is not what we are being told. Nor is this what we teach our children.

Instead, our children have been taught to worry when they are away from us. They panic when they cannot reach someone immediately. God forbid the battery on their phone runs out. Without access to a device, or someone responding right away, they automatically assume worst case scenarios. Being on their own, without their phone, is unimaginable. They have been trained to be hyper-vigilant to the notion that something could happen at any moment and therefore, they must remain in possession of a device at all times because after all, *Life itself is something to be afraid of.*

The cultural narrative that all is well, that our children are out of harm's way and living within the limits of our expectations of them just because they have a cell phone puts me in mind of the college student who left her cell phone in her dorm room when she went to stay at her boyfriend's for the night. *Why?* So that when her mother tracked her, it looked like she was where this mother needed her to be. Not only was a false sense of security created via a machine for this mother, an erosion of trust in their relationship was born as this young woman chose to be deceitful in response to the control being levied against her. There was a lost opportunity here for this college student to get to know and to decide her own mind. Her ability to stand on her own with confidence and to make decisions that only she could make is but one of the casualties here.

All because this mother put her fears and her worries above the developmental imperative that this young woman get a chance to cultivate her own agency. And because surveillance was favored over trust in this mother-daughter relationship, we can only assume what this may cost this young woman in terms of her capacity to trust herself.

Overuse Of The Safety Card

Evidence of our obsessive need to protect our children against ordinary life is everywhere now. We put helmets on kids learning to walk. We are uptight when they play outside. The monkey bars are not safe and neither is riding your bike to a friend's house down the block. This epidemic of obsessive protection that swings between infantalization and overprotection was exemplified each summer at my kid's elementary school. The school opened *daily* from 8 am to 2:30 for *the entire month of August* so that students could come in and practice their *locker opening skills* at the school's new Locker Learning Station.

If our children require this level of overkill to do something so basic, we are either seriously under-estimating our children, or something has gone terribly awry in normal human development. We overexpose them to destructive images and content they are far too young to handle via the shows and gaming we say yes to, while simultaneously over-scaffolding age-appropriate experiences. We over do and we under do. This has the effect of strangling the naturalness and the joy right out of their growing up. We are confusing knowing where they are and being able to reach them, with safeguarding them. Deluding ourselves and them while we deny a reality that will never, *ever* change: *Unplanned for, unexpected and difficult things to bear will most certainly happen in life with our children. Whether our children have a cell phone, or not.*

Without facing up to one of *the* harshest realities we as parents will ever have to be with, we risk deluding ourselves and our children. More to the point, we risk making choices that not only *do not* keep them safe, but that inadvertently bring unanticipated consequences, problems and dangers into their lives. We cannot always protect our kids and to pretend we can leaves us prey to ideas, devices and ways of living that offer a false promise of invulnerability and security. It is a most disturbing truth to recognize we cannot control Life on behalf of our children. But it is one we must face up to if we hope to avoid making potentially illusory and harmful choices in our attempts to keep our kids safe.

We use "safety" these days to justify all kinds of things with our children. And to challenge the safety card is to identify yourself as a bad or uncaring parent. For sure, there are realities, risk-assessments and trade-offs we must all make for our children. But we want to make our choices based on what is real, *versus what is imagined*. This is again where the practice of mindfulness becomes a powerful way to navigate through all of the hyped up and exaggerated fears. Being more present is what allows you to discern between what is real and what is made-up. This is the antidote to the fear-mongering and the catastrophizing that is so prevalent in the culture. The practice builds the lens of discernment to help you notice where there is a glitch in your understanding of safety and danger that may be undermining your capacity to see clearly as a parent.

For instance, the very same parents who obsess over keeping their kids safe are the very same ones who allow harmful elements into their homes through the screen technologies *every single day* in the forms of age-inappropriate content, violence, gratuitous sexuality and nonsensical images that dulls their child's body, mind and soul. Parents who attempt to bubble wrap their kids from the natural experiences of childhood are the same ones installing tracking systems and nanny cams based on unlikely scenarios. *Is this the legacy we want to pass on to our children?* One where they are simultaneously afraid of everything, while being prepared for so little because they have not gotten the chance to experience life without the alarm bells of the screens falsely and exaggeratedly signaling danger? You might be thinking that what's changed in terms of safety is that the world is more dangerous now. However, there is a lot of research that says we are living in a time where individual danger and violence against children is actually historically low. This stands in contrast to the collective agreement that danger lurks everywhere for our kids, and that if we are not micro-managing them through the technologies, we are not doing a good job keeping them safe.

The truth is, real safety begins at home. It begins with how you treat your children. It begins with what you allow them to be exposed to. *Do you allow violent forms of entertainment in your home? Do you protect your children from ideas, words and images that are beyond their ability to comprehend, and that violate their innocence? Is your home free from violence?* This goes beyond the obvious understanding of not beating up on your children and includes name calling, aggressive or disrespectful language, put downs and harmful sarcasm. It also extends to how safe your children feel to be who they truly are. Free from harmful criticism of their choices, friends, style or their interests. In our attempts to guard against some boogeyman "out there," we often miss the predator within; either the one that lives within us, or the one we let in through the screens. Creating safety is *never* about anxiously binding our children to us. Or for that matter, to a piece of machinery.

Teens And Driving

A reflection on safety would not be complete without looking at teens and driving. One of the number one reasons why parents feel their children need a cell phone is when they begin to drive. Driving is an inherently risky endeavor, more so for new drivers. Research says the number one way our teens die an accidental death is in a car crash. *And* that the number one cause of these crashes is distracted driving. Guess what the number one distraction is? *Cell phones.*

In our attempt to believe we can minimize or eradicate the risks associated with driving, we have created not only more risk, but the very scenario we are trying desperately to avoid. Which begs the question: **How smart is it to put your teen in a car with a cell phone?** How smart is it to give an immature, cognitively undeveloped and impulsive human being an item so persuasive in its ability to grab their attention, that they just cannot say no to its call? No matter what you have told them. No matter what they have promised you. No matter what all the new apps guarantee you.

We make laws that say they must have six months of driving experience under a junior operating license before they can have friends in the car because we know what a distraction this is to them. *Why are we not enforcing the same types of conditions regarding the cell phones?* Although the law says you can't text and drive, talk to any teen who is not your own kid and ask them what they are up to in this department. I regularly heard from college students that they know it is bad to text and drive, *BUT* they just happen to be the one who is *really good* at it. This logic smacks of the very same justification that people drinking and driving will often give in terms of how proficient they are at driving under the influence, when in fact, they are horribly impaired.

If you feel that for "safety" reasons a cell phone is something you would like your child to have, here are a couple of things to consider. One, this is a choice, a preference, something you would "like," but **not** an absolute require-ment, and **never a guarantee of safety.** This is a luxury, and as such it should be kept in its place. If you are old enough to drive a car, you are old enough to problem solve and be resourceful all on your own. Two, if it truly is about safety, why then do our children need smart-phones? *Why encourage the distraction?* Why purchase something with all the bells and whistles which begs them to be distracted while driving? How does this help insure your child's safety? *It does not.* If you feel strongly they need something, make it utilitarian. They may hate it, but you will have established yourself in the position of the one who understands the risks far better than they, and as the one who is willing to act on behalf of that knowing.

The Issue Of Friends

The role that cell phones play in our children's lives would be incomplete without looking at how the over-intrusion in childhood of the devices is harmfully impacting their ability to meaningfully and successfully navigate relationships. This is another one of those areas where we have been blinded by our fears. The fear in this area being that without a device in their possession, our children will be friendless.

This fear strikes deep at the heart of any parent. For many of us being the most unimaginable and unwanted thing we could ever hope to have happen to our kids. Which is why we are so susceptible to missing the truth: *When and where it is that the cell phones are actually damaging their social skills and leaving them prey to harmful exchanges.* Real human contact is being thrown aside for machine-mediated interactions. Their ability to understand and handle the nuances of relationships is worsening because of it. Despite all their "connectedness" they are lonelier, less satisfied, more stressed, more neurotic, and at times, even suicidal.

Our social relations are precious. One of *the most precious* aspects of being alive. We need each other. We need to know that we can count on one other. We need to know that we matter to each other. Something this important in the life of a human being deserves your attention, nurturance and protection. Which is why it is so interesting to observe how willing we have been, in a very short amount of time in the evolutionary span of our species, to let its importance be overshadowed by something that is not even human. All because we are afraid that without it, our kids won't have friends.

What's essential to point out here is that healthy social connections don't just mean friends. Our social skills serve as the very foundation for lifelong health, happiness, job success, lifetime satisfaction, fulfillment and more. The development of this skill is an ongoing, sensitive and easily derailed process. To tamper with it is to leave your children at a loss across all areas of their lives; physical, mental, emotional and spiritual. Which speaks to a deeper contemplation around why we allow the phones to do the work in our relationships. I think it's because cultivating healthy relationships is one of the most difficult things a human being will ever be asked to do. And I think we are terrified because we're so afraid of what it actually takes to build true intimacy.

Maybe this is why our children might "tell all" in a post or tweet but not in person; believing they have engaged in a healthy disclosure because they have hit the publish button. Maybe it is why texting versus speaking in person feels less threatening; more manageable, known and controllable. Look around and you will see how accustomed we have become to hiding behind our technological walls; somehow feeling more protected, less exposed and more insulated against the pitfalls of being in relationship.

But as with anything that blocks learning a skill, the more we allow into their lives something that eliminates the need to develop their social skills, *the worse they get at doing it*. Until they are not even doing it all. Which is exactly what we're seeing so much of now. Device in hand, our children are learning the wrong things in their early forays into relational life—leaving them sorely unprepared to actually maintain healthy connections with others. Let's face it, relationships are sometimes awkward, difficult, confusing and messy. Part of our children's social growth curve is to learn how to weather challenging and uncomfortable times with other people; without hiding out, curating or ghosting.

Hiding behind a screen is not communicating. Texting is not a conversation. An emoji is not a heartfelt expression of affection. A period at the end of a text is not an angry response. Responding immediately to a text is not an indication of a good relationship. Waiting to respond is not the sign of a brush off. Neurotically texting one another across the day is not a sign of commitment or devotion. ***The ability to text, call or send child-like cartoonish expressions of our affection is not the measure of a relationship well tended.*** Despite the meaning all these things have been given, they are no more than an anti-social agreement among us that has done nothing to further our connection to one another. Our children are being misled about what makes for lasting and satisfying relationships; believing that an obsessive stream of texts equals safety and closeness

The vast majority of human communication is non-verbal. No wonder there is so much confusion and dissatisfaction in our screen exchanges. Everything that brings nuance and meaning is alarmingly absent—leaving our exchanges more machine-like, and less human. This certainly explains all the miscommunications that occur across a text. And it stands as a solid argument for not allowing a cell phone to degrade a child's growing capacity to understand non-verbal communication. Not to mention how the self-obsession epidemic known as "selfies" has created a culture of narcissistic, entitled, self-indulgent and insecure people. How will that contribute to a satisfying relationship? *It will not.*

Final Words: A Reality Check

When I was pregnant with my first baby, I read a book on health and healing that recommended doing a news fast. I had two reactions. I thought it was ridiculous. And I was intrigued. At the time, I was a news junky. I watched the news in the morning and at night. I listened to the news on the radio on my way to work, and I read all the popular magazines distilling down the news of our times. *And I feared for my safety.* I imagined worst case scenarios about being harmed or raped. I saw danger lurking everywhere. I regularly conjured up ideas about bad people who were out to get me. You might imagine then my total surprise at noticing how after just one week of a news fast, how much more at ease I felt in the world. More safe. More at home.

It felt so right that I kept going. And I have never looked back.

Since then, I am extremely judicious about what I will watch, read or listen to because not only did I immediately feel better, I began to notice a kind of instinct, a sixth sense if you will, about situations and people arising in place of the fear; giving me all the information I ever needed to keep myself safe. This was different from trying to protect myself by obsessing on morbid deadly fantasies. A distorted perspective I might add that does nothing to keep you safe, wrecks your sense of wanting to be part of the world and undermines, by association, your children's capacity to develop an accurate sense of safety and danger.

Because my mind is no longer filled with all of the scary content coming across a screen, a solid relationship to the reality of Life has been born. One that is based on the truth of the moment, as opposed to imagined and self-generated fears and anxieties. One that arises from my unerring mammal nature that is quick to arise and is based on real environmental cues, instead of made-up stories. One that understands more clearly what I have control over, *and what I do not*.

And one that understands there are no guarantees in Life and to build my world view on that false assumption is to suffer, is to make choices based on made-up information and is to, ultimately, mislead my children.

We must remember that protecting our children, and projecting irrational fears onto them, is not the same thing. Because it feels like our children's well-being hangs in the balance, it can feel very, very risky to try and distinguish between the two. When we imbue the cell phones with an all-protecting power they do not possess because we are attempting to sidestep the necessary work of discerning fact from fiction, we pass on to our children a false sense of assurance in a world that offers no such guarantees. In the meantime, important life skills are not being developed. Couple this with the experience of being regularly saturated with fears and we have the recipe for destroying our children's sense of competency and well-being; leaving them with ill health, mental instability, a lack of common sense, a disconnection from essential survival instincts, infantilized dependence and a lowered capacity to relate in person in real time in satisfying ways.

An Inquiry:
Faith

Why do we expect our loved ones to respond immediately *to us throughout the day?* Why is it that we cannot fathom leaving a little space in between our communications? Have we come to believe there is so little holding us together that we must repetitively and neurotically keep checking in with one another?

In our "never out of contact" world, just because you can text your child does not mean that you should. Trust, time and the space for them to figure things out on their own, while being in connection with a stable adult, is what they need from us. Not incessant and obsessive texting, checking, tracking and intervening. Even though it might feel loving and well-intentioned on your part, **when is it that you are confusing your ability to monitor and contact your child with what makes for a world-ready kid and a strong and healthy relationship with you?**

A crucial part of growing up is the experience of separating from your parents, establishing your own identity, and ultimately choosing your own life. It is a long-term, natural foray into more and more pockets of time of our kids being on their own. One that begins when your child first crawls away from you, and ends when they finally leave home. This gradual moving away is the training and proving ground for when they finally and fully separate. It requires countless, natural, real life opportunities throughout every age to successfully navigate the transitions that become available at different times and stages of their life. Experiences that cannot be artificially created or talked about.

This natural progress toward independence stands in stark contrast to the college students who would tell me they would "hear" from their parents multiple times a day, and that for many, if they did not respond *immediately*, their parents would push the panic button—automatically assuming something was wrong. Lost in their own fears, these parents had not factored in the reason there was no response from their young adult child was because they were in class. Or in a meeting. Or at a practice. Or maybe just not wanting to be interrupted. *Or god forbid, just wanting to be on their own without parental intrusion and interference.*

Spend some time inquiring into your own motivations for doing what you do in this regard. Include imagining how this is impacting your child's healthy development.

A Practice:
Reflecting On Your Use

What do you expose yourself to in terms of screen content? Do you feed yourself on a regular diet of doubt and fear as sold by the media? **Have you ever noticed the relationship between what you watch and how safe the world feels to you?** Research over the years has shown that the more TV one watches, the less safe the world feels to them. Pay attention to how tense and stressed you feel before, during and after time in front of a screen. The images and the information you take in creates your ideas about the safety or the dangers of the world. Across a screen, there is seemingly no end to the narrative that there are bad things happening everywhere, and that it is only a matter of time before it will happen to you, or *your child.*

This alone is a profound mindfulness practice. This is never about making things bad, but instead about giving yourself some breathing room to see how what you are being exposed to is impacting your level of fear when it comes to being a parent. Practicing in this way gives you a clearer picture around how what you ingest by way of the screens informs your levels of fear. Initially, don't change anything. Just watch yourself and how it is that you respond to screen content. This alone is all the guidance you will ever need to help you discern fact from fiction for both you and your children.

Potent Questions

When it comes to raising our children, we must begin with ourselves. They look to us and want to be like us. If you yourself see your phone as all-important, a kind of safety-savior even, *so will they*. If you put your phone ahead of your own capacity to navigate your environment, *so will they*. If you talk or text while you are driving, *so will they*. While they will certainly be influenced by others who have cell phones, we must never underestimate the power of the modeling that occurs from parent to child.

- *Do your children get the impression that what is happening on your phone is more important than them?*

- *Do you use your phone to create and support a reactive, chaotic life?*

- *Are your fears founded in reality or something you make up based on past experiences, future worries, or based on what you watch?*

- *Instead of monitoring your child's every move, what could you do to help them become more resourceful and independent?*

- *Where are the devices hampering your child's ability to learn judgment, communication skills, resourcefulness and personal responsibility?*

- *When is your child in all actuality more at risk with a device in hand?*

Practical Go-To's

Use the suggestions below to help you connect to the real realities of Life.

- **Learn how to assess real risk.** This requires your presence and your willingness to become aware of the unfounded fears you harbor.

- **Teach your children to pay attention to their surroundings.** Not out of fear or anxiety, but as a mother animal would instruct her baby on learning their surroundings.

- **Give your children every day simple opportunities to be resourceful.** Stop doing so much for them. Let them figure some things out on their own.

- **Never be on your phone while you're driving.** Hands-free or not. A kind of tunnel vision occurs when you're on your cell phone. Meaning, *there's lots you don't see.*

- **Ask "What for" instead of "What if."** Instead of worrying your way into a cell phone, look at the pros and cons of assuming that possessing a cell phone is the solution.

- **A cell phone without a plan can still dial 911.** If it *really is* about safety, this is an option.

- **If you must, get them *just a phone.*** Nothing "smart."

- **Lay out the consequences.** Be clear and decisive in your response should your child use their phone while driving.

- **A stop gap.** Be up front with your child about your right to check their phone. *This is not the real work, but instead a stop gap measure.* Spying erodes your relationship.

- **No cell phone isolation.** Not in the bedroom at night, not as a way to isolate, and not in the car with you.

- **Lean into what we already know.** If you doubt that it's possible for children to be okay without a cell phone, we already know that it is.

- **Get a watch and buy an alarm clock.** These are two great ways to take cell phone use out of the equation.

- **Take the attitude:** *It is just a phone.* Act and live accordingly. It is not a friend. It is not the 5th limb. It is not the antidote to loneliness, unhappiness or boredom.

- **Consider a house phone.** When your child's friends have to call your home and go through you, an essential filter is established that's good for all involved.

Question everything.

9

Questioning Your Reality

"The frames our minds create define and confine what we perceive to be possible. Every problem, every dilemma, every dead end we find ourselves facing in life, only appears unsolvable inside a particular frame or point of view. Enlarge the box, or create another frame around the data, and problems vanish, while new opportunities appear."
Rosamund Stone Zander & Benjamin Zander

My younger brother died just before his thirtieth birthday. The experience of losing someone so young and so close to me cracked something open in me. It was no longer possible to go on with my life as usual. It was more than "just" grief I was experiencing. It was as if I had entered this place, this never before experienced reality, where everything got turned upside down. A world view I had held for more than three decades about how things would go, came crashing down. For months I couldn't believe, given what I was going through, that other people went on as usual. It was so hard to fathom how to be in this alternate reality where things no longer lined up as they once did. It was during this time period that for the first time in my life, an awareness of what it was that mattered most, began to make itself known to me.

Not long after my brother died, I was out on a walk thinking about him, as I often did. These walks were my way of trying to sort through all that was happening. Part of the sorting was a wondering on my part about him. He had known for quite some time he was going to die. As I thought about what that must have been like for him, I realized that despite all the difficult emotions, fears, regrets and more, there was also incredible freedom in knowing your time here is limited. Because he knew his life was coming to an end, somewhere along the way he had made the decision to let go of a lot that used to greatly occupy him. There was so much he had stopped caring about. There were so many models of "reality," ones he had held for his whole life about who he was and what was important, that he had let go of.

It was on one particular walk, that I began to imagine what my life would look like if I knew I only had six months to live.

This was something I was contemplating the following day as I entered the building where I was doing my doctoral internship. It was at this exact moment that my "six-month-rule," as I have come to know it, was born. As I stood between two sets of automatic doors, I knew if I only had six months to live, I would turn around, *without hesitation*, and walk out the door. I would not even go in to tell my supervisors I was leaving. That was how little the doctoral chase had come to mean to me. But because I had bought into the "reality"—mine and everyone's around me—that this was important, was what defined me, was what would give me value in the world, along with how I would be the first in my family or my husband's to be a doctor, I kept going.

I did not turn around that day. But several years later, I did. Though it took some time, I finally mustered the courage to let go of what I had bought into that wasn't working for me. A momentous moment in time that I spoke of earlier, where I stopped contributing to a reality that was not only limiting me, it was keeping me from what was most important to me. Although it took time to release the old model of reality, and for me to catch up to my new model, catch up I eventually did. But it never would have happened if I had not challenged a long-standing world view that told me what I needed to be doing, and how I needed to be doing it.

Having the willingness to entertain a new version of myself and my life, outside of my existing belief system, set me up for the life I was born to live. From that point on, the six-month rule became my guiding light—creating a template for how to shift my perceptions of myself and the world. This approach has challenged and stretched me in ways almost unimaginable. Difficult as it has sometimes been though, I would not trade a single challenge along the way. Learning to let go of old ideas and beliefs has allowed me to understand what it takes to be the author of my own life; gifting me with the immense rewards of personal meaning, satisfaction, peace, authenticity, fulfillment and truth. The very things my children most needed to see in me.

Shifting Realities

We create our realities, and therefore our lives, moment by moment. We weave together stories in our minds and with one another we refer to as "truth." Our stories, knowingly and unknowingly, tell us what is likely, possible and real. We gather these stories from our families of origin, our schools, our churches, the times we're living in, the books we read, the media we consume, our own personal and unique experiences, and so very much more. Contrary to what many of us believe, there is no *something* or *someone* out there that determines our lives. *We* determine our lives, and by extension our children's, based on what we choose to believe in.

Have you ever stopped to deeply question the "realities" you have bought into? This is a big ask. The biggest ever. Truly, a lifetime endeavor. Which is why I think so many of us never take it on because it means letting go of the ways we unconsciously hand over our lives to others; the government, teachers, politicians, streaming services, other parents, our family of origin, social media and even our own children. And yet, without this level of questioning, an essential aspect of being a parent who can grow and change in response to what is needed to properly care for and guide their children, becomes unavailable to us.

The good news is, we have already stepped in and out of holding different world views, many, many times across our lives. Think back on the fantastical things you once believed in as a child. Things you "knew" with certainty were true. *What happened to those childish beliefs?* You had to let them go in order to move on to a more mature understanding of Life. There is nothing wrong with holding models of reality that cease to be true over time. There is nothing wrong with coming up with ways of trying to explain and understand the world, and the things we do not yet comprehend. That is what makes us human. It is what organizes us. It is what helps us to know how to live. It is what gives us a structure to hold onto as we try to make sense of things that are often beyond making sense of.

But as we grow, we must have the courage to realize when the frames of reference we're using are limiting us and taking us in the wrong direction. That's why it's so important to get in the habit of cross-checking what you hold as true; recognizing when the realities you cling to are out of date, missing crucial details, or sometimes, *even flat out wrong.* And then, perhaps hardest of all, go on to uncreate what no longer holds up as you recreate something more true. More complete. More thoroughly vetted. While not an easy thing to do, it is our only recourse if we have any hope of meeting Life on its own terms. Otherwise, we are like an immature child, clinging to the idea that there is a Santa Claus. The parallel here being, holding onto the belief that the technologies are all about progress, even when we see evidence revealing to us that perspective is neither real nor true. That just like Santa Claus, it is a fantasy.

Charting A Course For Our Children

The most powerful and significant developmental shift we can make in our growth as a parent is learning how to make decisions from the inside-out, versus the outside-in. This goes well beyond the traditional markers of becoming a grown-up, where we have been led to believe that getting a degree, holding down a job, paying bills, buying a house and getting married are the truest reflections of becoming an adult. All of these are things we do, but they do not necessarily align with a kind of inner agency that is truly the hallmark of being a grown-up. What I'm talking about here has everything to do with how we take up the authorship of our own lives when it comes to what and why we choose what we do for our own children. This requires understanding we create, *and have had created for us*, mental models of reality about everything we do when it comes to the choices we make for our kids. And that it is up to us, *and only us*, to vet which models we will subscribe to. *Along with those we won't.*

We have models for what children need to be healthy, safe and successful. We have mental concepts about what makes for a good or a bad kid. We hold strong frames about how our children's lives must unfold in order for them to be okay. This includes how much screen time needs to be a part of their upbringing in order to belong and be prepared for the 21st century. It includes the number and types of devices we feel they must have. And it includes the content we believe is appropriate for them. This is all necessary and normal to have something to refer to when you are deciding what to do. The trouble though comes in when we live with these self- and culturally-generated concepts as if they were absolute and irrefutable truths, without challenging the origins, the agendas and the motivations behind them. Bound by the limitations of our unrecognized and unchallenged beliefs, we unwittingly leave our children unprotected when it comes to things like the devices they carry around as if it were the most necessary and normal part of being a human being.

Our perspectives about child raising are based on opinion, reaction, convention, habit, generational influence, cultural mandates and peer pressure. The child-rearing models we subscribe to now are influenced by our family of origin, the society we live in, who we associate with, the times our children are born into, school policies, political administrations, what we read, what we watch, our own fears, personal hang-ups, insecurities and so much more. And while these models of reality may feel solid and true for us, in actuality they are based on an ever-changing story that shifts with time, place, perspective and trends.

It seems only reasonable then that in order to serve our children well, *we must learn* to be conscious about the models we subscribe to on their behalf. At their very best, these are world views built with the end in mind, are based on real childhood needs and include the very best of what we have to offer while standing on time-honored traditions; ones that are not fickle to the times, marketing campaigns, pressures or anything else outside the real needs of our kids. Constructing and deconstructing your world view takes a lot of courage and self-confidence. It also requires a kind of inner sacrifice you make on behalf of your own children where you allow yourself to be relieved of those things that are out of date. *And even untrue.* Thinking like this takes time and practice. It demands we tap into more timeless truths regarding human nature and what developing beings most need.

In the end, it will always call for us to travel beyond the outmoded beliefs, distractions and the external demands of modern life, navigating instead by what it is that most serves the living, breathing life of our child.

Learning To Proceed With Caution

I'd like to take the time now to introduce The Precautionary Principle: A way of approaching the decisions we make with more of a "wait and see" attitude. That when something new to the species, like the technologies, enters our world, or more specifically, enters the life of our child, we choose a "guilty until proven innocent" perspective. We already do this in many domains. We already understand the value of waiting and of protecting our children from experiences they are not developmentally ready for. Getting a driver's license, drinking, voting, getting married, leaving school, deciding medical issues or serving in the military are all examples of us understanding there are certain experiences in life that require a level of physical, emotional and cognitive maturity that our children do not yet possess. And so, *we wait.* For instance, we don't allow a four-year-old to drive a car because that would be to ignore their lack of judgment and physical capacity. We do not let a seven-year-old marry because that would be to ignore their lack of emotional and relational readiness. We do not send a ten-year-old off to war because that would be to traumatize them on every level of their being. To open our children up to too soon, too much and too often when it comes to exposing them to the virtual world before they are developmentally ready, is no different.

In the spirit of The Precautionary Principle, what if we put warning labels on the various devices that listed out the side effects? What if technology commercials had to do what the pharmaceutical commercials are required to do by providing health warnings listing out all of the known side-effects? Under these circumstances, would we still be so quick to equip our children with a device?

- **Warning:** Known to cause addictive behavior.

- **Warning:** Use associated with anxiety, depression, insomnia and suicidal ideation.

- **Warning:** Isolation and a reduction in meaningful relationship time is to be expected.

- **Warning:** A decreased interest in reading and any other activities which require sustained attention and concentration.

- **Warning:** May cause eye strain, difficulty sleeping, postural problems, repetitive stress injuries and more.

- **Warning:** May lead to a sedentary lifestyle resulting in weight gain, obesity, diabetes and heart disease.

- **Warning:** Use may result in DNA disruption, cancer and changes in brain functioning.

- **Warning:** Not for children. Or to be used without a grown-up present.

Would you allow anything else into your home that had even one of these warning labels on it? The screens technologies are marketed and sold as not only desirable, *but risk-free.* Growing research, personal observation and common sense wisdom tell us *this is just not true.*

What if, when it came to the screen technologies, we developed some foresight and started living as if the needs of people and Life itself were our most important priorities? With corporate America, "convenience," and peer pressure, along with the need to prove how progressive we are, ranking way down on the list. *Maybe not even making the list.*

The Convenience Trap

While there are many reasons many of us have bought into the "reality" that our kids need the devices, the belief that the screens make our lives more convenient has gone mostly unchallenged. Somehow, without a lot of us questioning it, convenience has been elevated to such a status that we have ignored much we never should have. Like how disorganized, overly busy and chaotic our lives have become due to the presence of the cell phones. We over-schedule and we push too hard. We dash from one commitment to another; barely making it in time to where we need to go next. Only to get up and do it again. Under these conditions we *absolutely* require the technologies front and center to manage our family's lives. But at what point does *the very presence of the devices themselves*, allow, encourage, *and even demand*, that we live at such an inhumane tempo?

While we often imagine that the devices help to keep our lives more manageable, the truth often reveals that possessing a cell phone allows us to be more reactive, disorganized and chaotic then without one. For instance, with the phone, we can be very last minute. We can fail to make a solid plan. We can cram way more into a day than is good for a human being. We can sign our kids up for way too much and we can be terrible at time management. And we can live as if Life itself is an emergency we are just barely surviving.

Just because you can do more does not mean it is good for you, or in the best interest of your children. One of the most important realities you can examine is whether or not your life is truly better with the technologies and how it is you are using them. While it may be true in some regards that things are better, *where it is not true?* If we're going to live with integrity around the models of reality we rely on, the very ones we pass on to our children, we must be willing to include as full of a picture as we can when it comes to something this seductive and this collectively agreed upon. Being part of the groupthink on this one, while offering an easy world view to step into, does not necessarily offer you and your family solid guidance or support for what matters most to you. Meaning, that even though the cultural narrative has been how much better and more convenient our lives are, does this ring true for the way your life actually feels?

The Call Of The Collective

To challenge existing and collectively held realities requires digging deep into your values. What do you really want for your children? What kind of people do you hope they become, and what is it they need in order to get there? Look as far into the future as you can, beyond even the places where your ideas and projections end, and their life, separate from you, begins. *What do they truly need to live the life they are most meant to live?* Only by asking these kinds of questions can you begin to consider where, in your model of reality, that the technologies fit, and where they do not. Only then can you begin to consider whether the reality you subscribe to is even yours, or one that was handed down to you that you've never really questioned.

The reality is, we are social creatures and for our biological and emotional health and well-being, we require affiliation with others. That's why it can feel inconceivable to imagine operating differently than those around you. It can even feel dangerous psychically or physically, or like a kind of social suicide, to move against the social "realities"of our times. Which is why the biggest and most difficult paradigm shifts to be made often involve those where you decide differently than those around you. Perhaps nowhere is this more essential than the decisions you're making around the downside of the technologies in childhood. There has been a kind of collective blind spot when it comes to admitting this. But if as parents we can learn to make choices different from those around us, while at the same time leaning into what the culture offers *that is* supportive, nourishing and life-affirming, our capacities as human beings, along with the health and vitality of our communities, expands for the benefit of all. This way of being becomes something we can pass on to our children. Truly, there is nothing more empowering for an individual, and ultimately nothing more beneficial for the group, than a person who knows who they are and what it is they stand for.

This means finding a balance between our individual needs, wants and desires, and the call of the collective. It means learning when and for what reasons to go with the herd, and when and for what reasons to strike out on our own. Discerning when it is more powerful to accept cultural norms and do things as the group does, and when it is we must reject what is being offered to our kids that we know is not in their best interest. This is truly the proverbial razor's edge. An edge that continuously shifts and changes with time, circumstances and our growing understanding around how to walk the balance between the needs of a growing child and the demands of the culture.

Final Words: A Model Of Your Own

It has been a truly affirming experience to have been writing out all these personal stories while I reflected back over twenty years. As I look at the themes that run through this book, so many have to do with me finding my own way as a parent. With me critically looking at and challenging the models of reality I had been given, in favor of what actually aligned with my values, my dreams and my vision of what is possible for us all when we really tune into what people require.

I know one thing for certain: When it has come to my capacity to sort truth from fiction around the world views I hold, it would never have been possible without two things: Regular time on my own, and a willingness to be open to world views that were dramatically different from mine. Traditions like Yoga, Ayurveda, Shamanism, Alternative Health and Healing, Food as Medicine, Meditation, Sacred Dance and more. Each one grew, challenged and empowered me in the most inspiring of ways. Without getting out of my comfort zone on a regular basis by subjecting myself to different narratives, my mind would never have been able to open up to the myriad of possibilities available to me when it comes to the realities I reference.

How we frame the times we are living in matters. What we name something matters. It sets the stage for what we value, what we want, what to expect and what to believe in. It tells us what is "normal." The words we use are extremely powerful when it comes to creating our models of reality. So while we use phrases like *Cyber Life*, *The Digital Age*, *The Age of Technology*, is it truly in the best interest of the human race to define ourselves in relation to machines? Why don't we define ourselves in relation to our humanity? Or how conscious we can be? Or how about a grand vision of the world we most want?

An Inquiry:
The Value Of Skepticism

Yes, the screens do things for us we cannot do on our own. Yes, they leave us feeling more powerful, competent, secure and connected. Yes, "everyone" has one, so we want one too. And yes, the devices have made things easier, faster and more convenient. They thrill and they entertain. Not to mention we've been told the technologies will give our children a leg up academically and in their ability to be successful in the world. All of this, of course, is one model of reality around the role of the screens and what it is our children need to be happy, connected and successful.

But if we want to open fully to the complete reality around life with the technologies, we are obliged to question more deeply. Certain wild animals, coming upon food they have never encountered before, will take only the smallest of bites to test things out. Like the wild animal encountering something for the very first time, might we be well-served to take very small nibbles of the technologies—while giving lots of time to digest before going back for more? Might we be better served by learning to balance our initial thrill with a healthy dose of skepticism and caution?

If you were to take a more skeptical approach, what might it look like in your life? *How might you use a life-giving skepticism on behalf of your family?* To ask these questions is to be willing to slow down long enough to contemplate some very difficult questions. For instance:

What are the health risks of the technologies in childhood?

What is being lost when the devices occupy so much of your children's time?

What is happening to their right to privacy?

Questioning like this means taking a more conservative approach in the midst of a culture that is always pushing for more, faster and earlier. It means getting clear on your values, your kid and what it takes for you to be more present. It requires getting clear on what constitutes harmful forms and uses of the technologies. And it requires a willingness to learn some very, very good reasons for saying "No" and "Not Yet." *No. It is not good for you. No. All of the information about how this will impact you in the future is not yet in. No. You are far too precious for me to take that chance. No. That is not how we do things as a family. Not yet. You are still too young for this.*

A Practice:
What Do Kids Actually Need?

One way to get started in challenging the models of reality you subscribe to is to start exploring whether or not what you believe is true. There are many ways to approach this. Leave space in your schedule to sit with your own thoughts. Structure reflective conversational times with a partner or friend to give yourself the room to speak your own thoughts and feelings in the company of someone you trust. Pay attention when you feel triggered by someone believing differently than you do to see if there is something to be learned. Write out your beliefs and how you have come to believe them. Read authors whose writings encourage you to find your own voice. Seek out the lives of famous people whose viewpoints were different from the prevailing "realities" of their times to see if you can find instruction and inspiration from those ahead of you.

You could also use questions like:

Is it true my child needs a cell phone to be safe?

Is it true my child must be on social media to have friends?

Is it true they won't be able to entertain themselves?

Is it true that everyone needs their own device?

Is it true they will make my life miserable if I change the way we are doing things?"

Look through the lens of a lifetime. Whenever you are feeling stumped, imagine a time when your children are grown and the intensity of child rearing and all of its pressures have passed. *What will your regrets be?* Will any of those regrets have to do with your kid not getting a cellphone, video game or new app? Will you ever lament the fact that they did not have access to a device that kept them up late into the night, robbed them of creative pursuits, interfered with a satisfying social life or exposed them to inappropriate content? *Or will it be something else?*

Potent Questions

There is nothing more powerful than a simple, well-placed, out-of-the-box question to really shake up and reveal the beliefs we unthinkingly adhere to. The ones we don't challenge because either we do not know they are there, or because it feels too scary to do so. To wonder about something begins to soften the hard edges of our old and entrenched perspectives, opening us to new ones. In that spirit, have you ever wondered…

- *If children really need technology early and often in their lives to be academically successful? Who says so? What's their agenda?*

- *If it is actually true that our children won't have friends if they aren't on social media?*

- *What would happen if the grown-ups banded together around children and technology and agreed not to…fill in the blank?*

- *If your life really would be more difficult and arduous in the long run if your kids weren't so consumed by electronic devices?*

- *If it is a good idea to let corporations tell you what your kids need?*

- *If it is in the best interest of creating humane environments to have screens up everywhere we go now?*

- *If the technologies are making us more miserable?*

- *If there are dangerous health effects of the technologies?*

And have you ever wondered what you life would be like if your kids were well-rested, knew how to entertain themselves, were able to focus easily and naturally, were less argumentative, calmer, loved to be outside and preferred you over a machine? If you can imagine any of this, let that serve as the birthplace of a new model of reality. One that puts kids, your family and what you all really need first.

Practical Go-To's:

- **Question everything!**

- **Listen to your gut. Listen to your gut. Listen to your gut.**

- **Be brave for your children.**

- **Seek out people and resources who are doing things differently than you.**

- Connect to ancient, time-honored wisdom and ways of being that put people and the planet first.

- Deeply question any narrative coming from someone who is selling you something.

- Forcefully challenge any "reality" that undermines your child's humanity.

- Take the long view.

Let us together
re-imagine our lives
and the lives of our
children.

10
Remembering That
What We Do Matters

"Determine that the thing can and shall be done
and then we shall find the way."
Abraham Lincoln

This last story begins at the end of my own children's childhood — a time when I now have the vantage point of looking back over the choices my husband and I made raising our kids and making a home together. A time when I am no longer so caught up in the doing and the figuring out of it all, having raised my children into adulthood.

For twenty years, I pursued a very particular course of action with great dedication regarding the protection and nurturance of my children's lives; including their right to a childhood free from harmful images, content and beliefs. It is only recently though, that I have begun to see not only the specific impact that it made on us, but also the bigger picture.

For some mysterious reason, becoming a mother compelled me to dive deep enough below the surface of what the culture told me my children needed to be safe, have friends and be prepared for the 21st century, in order to get to a place where I could hear my own voice. To a place where I could discover my own instincts as the surest route to recognizing and protecting the truest needs of my children. This put me in an exquisite position to be able to act on their behalf. But to do so, I had to develop a fierceness in order to withstand judgment, ridicule, nay-saying and suspicion from others. Not to mention the demons inside my own head telling me maybe I didn't know what I was doing. Maybe I was depriving my children and leaving them unprepared for the world they were born into.

I see now that the intensity required to protect them was a double-edged sword; serving a vital and necessary function in their life, and at times creating a wedge between me and others. Although I gave my children something enduring to come home to, it did put a lot of pressure on them outside of our home in ways I may never know about. So while our house rules gave them a great foundation, at times, I know it also created a rub between them and the world. I pray that any of those challenging experiences taught them the value of living their most deeply cherished values and of the necessity of keeping their own counsel.

Because it took me many years to be able to voice what it was I was actually doing on their behalf, the steep learning curve I was engaged with, left me clumsy and inarticulate at times given the herculean effort I was involved in. But in the end, I would not change a thing. *Why?* Because I brought everything I had to creating a home where my children were allowed a childhood, where our family was a valued priority and where our lives together were lived at a sane and humane pace. Where real human needs were recognized and honored. Where I was present to my family. Where our values were front and center in our life. Where my children learned how to stand for something, even when it was hard. And where everyone knew they were always more important than machines, cultural pressures or going along to get along.

Big Picture Thinking

It's essential we wrap our minds around the fact we're in the midst of an unprecedented and far-reaching experiment on humanity. One that is daily being worked out on our children via the technologies. I know this is tough to hear. It's tough to write about. But if we don't start with the reality before us, one that has already proven to be dramatically re-shaping, and even warping, what it means to be human, how will we be able to protect our children?

How will we be able to live with ourselves?

The very life and well-being of our society is at stake. We do not five or ten years to act. *Sound extreme?* It is. *Hard to hear?* Absolutely. But this is what is being called for now; a kind of brutal honesty with ourselves and each other. One that recognizes our children's intellectual, physical, social, emotional and spiritual health is being dramatically impacted, *and not for the better.* That we have allowed corporate powers, governmental agencies, our fears and insecurities, as well as our kid's friends determine what is best for our children, when in fact, *that is our job.*

There is no doubt that an issue this large and all-consuming can leave us feeling as if we have no power to make a difference or to exact a change. But aren't there still some things in our lives that are worth fighting for, *no matter what the odds?* Things left in this world that are not for sale, and must never, *ever*, be negotiated, *no matter what?* And isn't the courage to stand in the face of such odds exactly what it takes to be a parent?

How it is that we will come to see, with the clarity and the vision required of us, the arguably questionable exchange that is being made with our children's lives through the ways we're allowing the technologies to play such a dominant and all-pervasive role in their childhood, will define who we are as a people. Given we have gone about as far as we can on this planet living as we do, the reality is, *things must change.* To know this is to see that how we're living is hurting us and our kids. The danger, of course, lies in believing that we can continue in our denial, ignorance and arrogance, and that somehow in the end, the machines we keep generating and turning towards, will save us. Will fix us. Will mend what we keep breaking. That somehow the screens will be able to do what we will not, and have not, been able to do. That somehow their presence will afford us guaranteed outcomes of health, success, happiness, ecological balance and connection. But if we're paying attention, we can already see this for the falsehood that it is.

On the other hand, we can choose to turn back towards our humanity through the experience of protecting our children. This carries with it the seeds of our greatest opportunity to come back to ourselves. And in so doing, to claim and to reclaim our humanity and what it is that we most value. Many traditions hold that in order to find ourselves, we must first be lost. That in order to know the light, we must also know the darkness. May it be so that this is as dark as we need to experience before we step back fully into the light.

A New Vision

As I see it, *the very heart* of this conversation we've been engaging in is nothing less than a re-imagining of our lives and the lives of our children. Difficulties, uncertainties, confusions and all. This means we need a new vision. One that includes what is possible, individually and collectively. One that puts people first. One that remembers the value of childhood. And one that invokes the sacred in our daily lives as the greatest reminder of our humanity. This is not about knowing everything or doing it "right." Instead, it is about making a commitment to what you value most, and then living that commitment day after day after day. *When you feel supported, and when you don't.* When others understand what you're going for, and when others are threatened by it.

We are talking about nothing less here than how we choose to live and love and relate and think and feel and be and want and work and create, and so very, very much more. We are talking about having the foresight to decide what it is that will be in charge of a human life: *us or a machine?* Us or modern-day distractions? Us or marketing gimmicks and strategies? Us or the latest upgrade?

Make no mistake about it, *what you do here matters.* These are huge and lasting choices we're making daily on behalf of our children. For when we decide to introduce a technology into our child's life, we are agreeing to things that may be obvious, things that may not be so obvious and things that may not be revealed until way down the road. So instead of us defining ourselves based on the destructive illusion as handed to us by The Age of Technology, what if we chose instead, to define ourselves as creators of The Age of Humanity? An era characterized by and known for its foresight, bravery and commitment to Life. A time where innocence is protected and our homes valued. A crucial period in history where enough of us decide to get out of believing that the technologies are more important, and instead, venture into figuring out how to remember and live what is most important to us.

If you can imagine this, let us put our hearts, minds, energies and spirits together to create lives worth living, in a world worth living in for all.

My love to you all.
May you have all that you need to be brave enough to take a stand on behalf of your child's childhood.

Be intentional

and be in charge.

Appendix

"The best relationship to technology begins with none."
Catherine Steiner-Adair

We love our how-to's and our lists, so here's one from me to you. Remember though, keep your values, the developmental needs of your child and the requirements of the moment front and center. If you are going to say "Yes," be sure you remain the one in charge, as opposed to letting the technologies usurp that sacred position. Practice where it's easy first, and build from there.

It all begins with you. Limit your time in front of a screen when your children are around. Your screen time impacts both you and them. Whatever influences you, influences your children. *Whatever you do, they will do.* Likely for the rest of their lives.

Be intentional and be in charge. Make technological choices *permission-based*, and set limits in age-appropriate ways. It is *your* job to hold the big picture. This is something your child *cannot* do on their own. Taking charge is an act of love and protection by someone who knows better. Establish your house rules and hold the line.

What are you really saying "Yes" to? If you're going to say "Yes," consider the long-term consequences. Ask yourself, *"Is it appropriate to the moment?" "Is it developmentally appropriate?" "Is it in line with my values?" "Is it interfering with something more important?" "Is it a compelling use of the technologies?" "Is there another way to do this?"*

Learn the value in saying "No" and "Not Yet." This is not done as a deprivation or because technology is "bad." Instead, saying "No" is one of the most life-affirming ways you can fully say "Yes" to your child's innocence, health, creativity and social development. When in doubt, employ the "Rule of 5." Will their disappointment or frustration matter in 5 minutes? 5 days? 5 months? 5 years? Saying "No" is never about putting them at a disadvantage, but about nourishing their humanity, which will *always* be what puts them at their *greatest* advantage.

If you must use a screen, do not ignore your children. If your children are around while you "must" be in front of a screen, pause and make eye contact. *Really look at them.* Tell them how long you will be on your device, *and stick to it.* And if you have been apart, and are seeing them for the first time all day, be available to them *first* for as long as need be before giving your attention to the screen.

Stop continuously checking. Notice when you are needlessly and obsessively handling and fondling your phone. Monkey see, monkey do.

Make technology a "no big deal" in your home. Do not allow it to be any more or less important than the toilet. Do not deify or demonize the screens. Work to know its place in your life for what it is; a tool.

Evaluate why you own what you own and what drives your choices. Be savvy and skeptical in your purchases. Be alert to the pull of constant upgrades. Before buying the latest technology *du jour,* ask yourself; *"Do I really need this?" "Can we make do with what we have?" "How will this change things in our home?"* Avoid impulse purchases. Before buying anything, sleep on it.

Consider more than your personal convenience, status or momentary whims. If you care anything about our earth and its future, look into the ways that the materials used and the disposal of the technologies is harming our planet; its water, its air quality, its soil, its people. Consider how self-indulgent it is to purchase redundant screens and unnecessary upgrades, with the erroneous belief that everyone needs their own device, without considering long-term planetary consequences.

Do not make technology easy to access. Tuck screens away from view. Do not allow them to dominate your living spaces. Do not leave devices open and "on" all the time.

Do not use technology as a reward. Either it fits the moment, what your child truly needs and your values, *or it does not.* Rewards can actually disincentivize your child from learning to appreciate the value in doing things for their own sake. Ill-placed rewards are often nothing more than a bribe and will keep your children from the good and satisfying feelings of learning how to do things for the intrinsic value of it. Life is not a video game dispensing points and charms. Do not train them to always be looking for something in return for doing what just needs to be done. Looking to get external rewards creates a very immature, unsatisfying and self-serving relationship to life. Bottom line? You elevate technology's status to very, *very* special when you use it as a reward. *Watch out for this one.*

Keep your children close when they are in front of a screen. When you do choose to say "Yes," instead of tuning out because they are occupied, TUNE IN! This is not the time to let down or stop being a parent. *Remain present.*

Set clear limits and enforce them consistently. When the answer is "Yes," keep your child's time in front of a screen focused and time-limited. DO NOT expect them to monitor themselves. *They cannot.* The screens are far too powerful and seductive for them. The fact they cannot pull themselves away is not an indication of disrespect, weak character or bad behavior. It is an indication of the strongly addictive nature of the medium (which by the way, is *always* reason enough to say no.)

Create special occasion times to say "Yes." When you use the screens consciously, as a way of mixing up the schedule, a momentary flight of fancy or as a shared experience, it can serve as a nice break from the routine. But when you make a life out of it, *that becomes a waste of life.* What if you were to take a page from the early TV viewers who saw it as a big deal; done for a very limited and specific amount of time while sharing the experience with others.

Homework. When your children are doing homework on the computer, help them by structuring it in ways so they are ONLY doing their homework; stay close, create time frames, limit the number of devices used at any given time *to one.* The length of time your children are doing homework *is not* an indication of their workload as much as it is a sign of the amount of distractions they get involved with online, and with their other devices. As your child hops from screen to screen, and window to window, their attention and focus must reboot each and every time to come back to their homework. The time spent re-focusing, plus all the diversions they are succumbing to, puts your child in front of a screen for unnecessary hours "doing homework." Translation: More exposure to radiation, less sleep, less downtime, less family and friend time, less time on their own and less living and relating in the real world.

Get involved with your school. Connect with your child's teacher by letting them know your thoughts on technology. Brainstorm with them to see if there are alternative ways to handle assignments. *Do not acquiesce to gratuitous and unconscious uses, even in the name of "education."* Talk with other parents at the school. Share your concerns. Set limits with other parents when your children are at their homes. While doing these things may be initially awkward or difficult, we must come together in our communities on behalf of our children.

Help your kids be successful. When you decide the situation warrants it and they are mature enough to handle what you are introducing them to (and you have spent years teaching them to check in with themselves), find ways to help your kids understand, and take responsibility for the consequences of their choices. This alone serves as an impeccable governor. For if your children are too immature to take this responsibility on, they are still too young to be handling what you are allowing. We already know this when it comes to voting, driving, drinking and more.

No to violent video games. *Ever.* Our world is being crushed under horrific and life-depleting levels of recognized and unrecognized violence against people and Nature. *Do not feed your children on this poison.*

"No" to anything for infants, toddlers and preschoolers. It is just not necessary. *Do not start them young.* The so-called "educational" software created by entertainment companies is not only unnecessary but false in its claims for making your child smarter or more ready for school. These apps do not give head starts, they waste your money and your child's precious childhood.

Do not let the screens babysit your child. Your child loses out on developing the necessary skills to self-regulate and entertain themselves when you regularly plug them in. Additionally, you sign yourself up for more fights, cranky children and extra effort on your part down the road. Put your time in up front with your children and both of your lives will shine because of it. While never easy, especially when you are tired or busy, your ability to structure your life in a way that includes them, as opposed to plugging them in, sends the message they have a place in your life. Learn to create a life together versus medicating them into silence.

There is nothing social about social media. Letting this one in your front door guarantees to sign your child up for more anxiety, depression, low self-esteem, learned social awkwardness and even suicide. This is pure poison when it comes to your child's social development and their long-term happiness.

Nothing at the dinner table. *Ever.* Your family needs this time to come together with nothing in between. Everyone needs a distraction-free and stress-free environment to properly connect with one another, while digesting nourishing foods in a mindful and relaxed way.

Nothing in the bedroom. *Ever.* Whatever your policies are, this just makes good sense for their sleep, their health, their innocence and their overall well-being. Leaving your child unattended in front of a screen, tucked away in their bedroom, opens them up to worlds beyond what they can handle, *despite what they might tell you.* Left unsupervised, you can count on them being up late into the night which opens them up to poor health, exposure to inappropriate content, moodiness and academic problems. And when they are tired, *everything* will be more difficult for them, *and for you.*

Downtime before bedtime. Create as big of a space as you can between screen time and bedtime. *For everyone.* Minimally a half hour, but more optimally 1-2 hours. The light being emitted, along with stimulating content will confuse the body's sleep wake-cycle and keep your child up long past their body's actual need for sleep. Everyone will fall asleep more quickly, sleep more deeply and awaken more refreshed. Who could ask for more?

Create screen-free times and spaces in your home. Take technology vacations on a daily and weekly basis. If you are always immersed in a sea of technology, you will not have the needed perspective that only its absence can offer. Without these absences, you will never have a clear picture of how the screens are *really* impacting your family.

Create a screen-free zone in your car. Consider including the car as one of your screen-free places. When you fill time in the car with cell phones and iPads, you are losing out on valuable opportunities to let down and to connect with your children. "Trapped" in the same time and space, you will be amazed at what comes up that just doesn't seem to arise at any other time. Open, agenda-free space together, where there is room for anything to evolve, is absolutely foundational to your relationship with them and to a child's healthy development. Do not miss out on this one.

Health. Creating wifi-free times and a no-devices-against-the-body policy gives everyone's body time to detox from damaging exposure to electromagnetic radiation. This is particularly important during sleep when your child's body is doing its healing and repair work. Growing bodies are far more susceptible to the impact of environmental toxins—radiation being one of them. Consider hard wiring your devices, or at least, turning the modem off at night. Never allow kids to have lap tops in their lap or cell phones in the "on" position against their body.

Designate an area for technology use and *stick to it.* Just as you have dedicated space for the kitchen or the bathroom, do the same with the screens. A desktop computer makes this easy as it stays in one place (as well as emits less radiation). You will have to be more disciplined with a laptop. No matter what you choose, limit use of the screen technologies to a specific spot in your home.

Keep designated screen space human. Have a window nearby to look out of. Create a great ergonomic set-up for the body. Place a beautiful picture or object between you and the screen as a reminder of your humanity. Place little reminder signs on the computer. Roll out a mat next to the screen for periodic body breaks. Keep water nearby. Avoid music, multiple screen use and anything else that prolongs time in front of a screen.

"Is this as good as it gets?" Regularly look around at your life and how you are using the technologies, wondering to yourself if this is, in fact, *actually* the good life.

Protect your child's humanity. Eliminate everything and anything that violates their humanity. This includes not only violence, but nonsense, adult material, time wasters, space fillers, avoidance generators, along with disrespectful and dysfunctional sexual content. Make human needs and your child's innocence a priority over technological addictions, fascinations and intrusions.

Eliminate anything that gets in the way of relationships. Whether that relationship is with themselves, family members, Nature, Spirit, or friends. *Anything* that interferes with satisfying and connected personal and relational time *needs to go*. Most especially, get it out of personally sensitive and rich relational times like right before bed, waking, after school, times when you are reconnecting with them after being apart, along with emotionally sensitive times.

Get committed and get creative. The possibilities of how you do or do not use technology in your child's life are endless once you get clear on your values, their needs and the priorities of the moment. Find ways to create a life where there is less need for your children to be in front of a screen. Have younger children's emails sent to you. When your child is writing a paper, unplug the modem, have them write it by hand or with a typewriter. When they have a question, encourage them to call the grandparents or a knowledgeable friend for the answer. Direct them to the library. Have spaces and materials in your home that offer everyone alternatives to the pull of the devices.

Get out the worst offenders. Get rid of everything and anything that gets in the way of safety, self-care, homework, chores, civil behavior, health, innocence, well-being and a positive and confident sense of self. Stop using the devices as background noise in your life. Stop letting your children and their friends focus on the screens as the way that they play and hangout. If it is health-depleting, soul sucking junk food for the body, mind or spirit, get rid of it! As surely as junk food will cause poor health, so too will junk technology.

Stranger danger. There are rules we all have about who we would let into our homes and whose company we want our children to keep. This must also hold true for the cast of characters who regularly enter your home via the screens. Evaluate what you are letting in and whether or not you would let what they are connecting to across a screen walk through your front door.

Balanced selections. Find media choices that inform versus alarm. Find alternatives that uplift and actually connect your family to something worthwhile. Help your kids savor the good in technology while differentiating and eliminating what is harsh, harmful and just pure rubbish. Develop a litmus test within yourself by asking, *"What is worthy of entering the sanctity of our home?"*

Provide a home filled with life and the living of it. Teach yourself to focus your family's life on what is most important. Real life is infinitely more multi-dimensional than the two dimensional virtual world. Machines can never offer what human beings truly need, *on any level.* Love and the joy of being alive is what puts the screens in their proper place. The devices pale in comparison to a life well-lived.

Acknowledgments

To Celia who helped me take an unwieldy number of pages and turn them into something.

To Leah for supporting me once again in making my thoughts a reality.

To Joanna for all the years you served as an impeccable sounding board for my rants and outrages around what was happening to our children via the technologies.

To Maddie and Jack for putting up with my little "experiment" in living. May the heart and soul of what I was trying to give you serve as a source of nourishment and protection.

To Steve who has been my co-creator through it all. May we continue to create a life based on what matters most to us. No matter what the world chooses to do.

And to The Good and Great Mother and to All those who have held me through the ups and downs of trying to get the word out. Thank you for all you have granted me.

About the Author

Susan McNamara, M.A., CHHC moved out to the woods of Western Massachusetts with her husband and two children with the aim of living closer to the land and closer to what it is that human beings actually need to thrive. For more than a quarter of a century she has been focused on living according to what matters most to her.

Susan has a Masters in Counseling Psychology and is trained and educated at the Doctoral level in Clinical Psychology. She is a Certified Holistic Health Counselor, Professional Level Kripalu Yoga Teacher, Journeydance Guide and Shamanic Practitioner.

www.RememberingWhatMattersMost.com